CHRIST'S DESCENT INTO HELL

Christ's Descent into Hell

John Paul II, Joseph Ratzinger, and Hans Urs von Balthasar on the Theology of Holy Saturday

Lyra Pitstick

William B. Eerdmans Publishing Company
Grand Rapids, Michigan

Published 2016 by
Wm. B. Eerdmans Publishing Co.
2140 Oak Industrial Drive N.E., Grand Rapids, Michigan 49505

www.eerdmans.com

Printed in the United States of America

22 21 20 19 18 17 16 7 6 5 4 3 2 1

Library of Congress Cataloging-in-Publication Data

Names: Pitstick, Alyssa Lyra, author.
Title: Christ's descent into hell: John Paul II, Joseph Ratzinger, and Hans Urs von Balthasar on the theology of Holy Saturday / Lyra Pitstick.
Description: Grand Rapids, Michigan: Eerdmans Publishing Company, 2016. | Includes bibliographical references and index.
Identifiers: LCCN 2015043019 | ISBN 9780802869050 (pbk. : alk. paper)
Subjects: LCSH: Jesus Christ — Descent into hell. | Holy Saturday. | Catholic Church — Doctrines. | John Paul II, Pope, 1920-2005. | Benedict XVI, Pope, 1927- | Balthasar, Hans Urs von, 1905-1988.
Classification: LCC BT470.P58 2016 | DDC 232.96/7 — dc23
LC record available at http://lccn.loc.gov/2015043019

The inscription in the 14th-century image on the cover reads (in Old French), "How the soul of Jesus has now, after death, descended into Hell and set free Adam and Eve and all the good who were in the ultimate prison. And He leaves all the bad, male and female, therein to abide in perpetual pain."
My thanks to Dr. Catherine Brown Tkacz for her help with this translation.

Dedicated to Mary, Queen of Heaven
and
St. Ignatius of Loyola and Company

For Fr. John Saward, Theologian

BY THIS CONSTITUTION which is to remain in force for ever,
we, with apostolic authority,
define the following: . . .

SINCE THE PASSION AND DEATH of the Lord Jesus Christ,
these souls [who "were not in need of any purification when they died . . .
or else, if they then needed . . .
some purification, after they have been purified after death,"
including "the souls of all the saints who departed from this world
before the passion of our Lord Jesus Christ"]
have seen and see the divine essence with an intuitive vision
and even face to face . . . ;
and in this vision they enjoy the divine essence.
Moreover, by this vision and enjoyment the souls of those who have already died
are truly blessed
and have eternal life and rest.

POPE BENEDICT XII,
Constitution *Benedictus Deus* (1336),
DS 1000

CONTENTS

LIST OF TABLES

ACKNOWLEDGMENTS

The core of this book reprises a lecture I gave at Heythrop College, London, May 9, 2011, funded by the Templeton Foundation as a result of my Templeton Award for Theological Promise (2009). I am deeply grateful to the Foundation for its *avant garde* willingness to recognize and so generously support junior theological researchers independently of institutional affiliation. May others do likewise! I extend very warm appreciation also to the Heythrop Jesuits for their gracious hospitality. Deserving of particular note in this regard is John Dade, S.J., Principal, for his invitation, enthusiastic participation, and comments, as well as Dominic Robinson, S.J., for his attentive management of the details of my visit and continuing collegiality. I am likewise warmly grateful to Gavin D'Costa of the University of Bristol for going above and beyond in laying the groundwork for my Templeton lectures in England and Scotland. Finally, I thank Hope College for a 2011 Nyenhuis Summer Research Grant, which partially funded the revision of the text, and I especially appreciate the generosity of the Betty S. Wheeler Trust, for a grant that enabled me to expand and finish it.

Feast of the Queenship of Mary
August 22, 2012

LYRA PITSTICK

NOTE TO READER

A date in parentheses after a title is the date of the text's publication or presentation in its original language, though the title of a non-English work may still be given in English.

Unless otherwise indicated, all quotations from papal documents are from the English versions on the Vatican website (www.vatican.va), and all translations from non-English publications are mine. Due to the dynamic nature of the Internet, readers may find pages have changed since the text here was completed.

Bible texts are from the *Revised Standard Version*, unless they are quoted from a cited source, in which case they are reproduced as quoted.

The author and publisher gratefully acknowledge permission to reprint material from the following sources:

Excerpts from the English translation of the *Catechism of the Catholic Church* for use in the United States of America. Copyright © 1994, United States Catholic Conference, Inc. — Libreria Editrice Vaticana. Used with permission.

Excerpts from *The Catechism of the Council of Trent,* transl. John A. McHugh, O.P., and Charles J. Callan, O.P. (Rockford, IL: Tan, 1982). Used with permission.

Text of *Benedictus Deus* reproduced from *The Christian Faith in the Doctrinal Documents of the Catholic Church,* 6th ed., ed. Jacques Dupuis (Staten Island: Alba, 1996).

Text of " 'He Descended into Hell': General Audience Given on January 11,

1989," by Pope John Paul II, transl. L'Osservatore Romano Weekly Edition in English. Copyright © 1989, LIBRERIA EDITRICE VATICANA. Reproduced with permission.

"The Passion and Triumph of Eternal Spring" was first published in *Gonzaga Witness* (April/May 2007): 16-17.

INTRODUCTION

Does the high regard of Pope (now St.) John Paul II and Joseph Cardinal Ratzinger (now Pope Emeritus Benedict XVI) for Hans Urs von Balthasar indicate approval of his controversial theology of Holy Saturday? Certainly Ratzinger uses some language similar to Balthasar's when discussing Christ's descent into hell, but does he mean the same thing by it? And what to do about the fact that both Ratzinger's and Balthasar's theologies contrast dramatically with John Paul II's? The radical differences in the three men's conclusions imply that not all of these influential theologians can be correct in what they say of Christ's descent.

But if one or more is wrong, who is it?

And what should we then make of John Paul II's and Benedict XVI's praise of Balthasar? If the popes lauded someone with whom they disagreed, did they err in praising him or in disagreeing with him? Could there be implications for papal infallibility? Or does their praise simply concern something other than the theological matter on which they disagreed?

And how might we go about answering these questions?

Balthasar has a reputation as a conservative theologian who explicitly understood his work as service to the Church. His name is closely linked with the renewed emphasis on the Church Fathers during the mid-twentieth century in what is called the *ressourcement* (return to the sources) movement. His writings make frequent reference to Scripture and leave an impression of staggering erudition. Henri de Lubac, no mean theologian himself, said

Balthasar was "perhaps the most cultivated man of his time."[1] Balthasar was a member, and then a priest, of the Society of Jesus (the Jesuits), remaining with them some twenty years, an experience that indelibly shaped his spirituality. Balthasar had a close friendship with Joseph Ratzinger, who eulogized him at his funeral in 1988 and, as Pope Benedict XVI, lauded him on the centennial of his birth. Earlier, John Paul II had conferred on Balthasar the first Paul VI Prize for his theological contributions and nominated him to be a cardinal. Especially for Catholic theologians, including myself, how could such a man's works be regarded as anything but trustworthy, apparently founded on Scripture and Tradition as they are, praised as they are by not one, but two, popes? Isn't papal judgment the standard of Catholic orthodoxy? Wouldn't it be hubris to try to "be more Catholic than the pope"?

After I raised questions about Balthasar's theology of Holy Saturday in 2007 with the publication of *Light in Darkness: Hans Urs von Balthasar and the Catholic Doctrine of Christ's Descent into Hell*, versions of this argument have consistently appeared in discussions of the book, most commonly in non-academic sources. The frequent, quick, and often vehement defenses of Balthasar on the web illustrated the degree of confidence people felt they could have in assuming Balthasar's reliability as a voice of Christian orthodoxy — and, apparently, how shaken some were by any suggestion he may have erred. Moments of unintentional humor in some hasty postings aside — one person wrote that he hadn't read *Light in Darkness*, but clearly I didn't know what I was talking about! — the argument's recurrence indicates it deserves an answer, especially as it would likely occur to any person, Catholic or non-Catholic, cursorily acquainted with Balthasar's place in theological history. Indeed, it weighed on my mind for a good part of my studies — until I looked more closely into it.

Except for one partial exposition by Edward T. Oakes in an article for the *International Journal of Systematic Theology*,[2] it is notable that the argument is universally made, regardless of venue, without considering exactly what

1. Henri de Lubac, "A Witness to Christ in the Church: Hans Urs von Balthasar," *Communio* 2, no. 3 (Fall, 1975): 230.

2. Edward T. Oakes, S.J., "*Descensus* and Development: A Response to Recent Rejoinders," *International Journal of Systematic Theology*, 13, no. 1 (January, 2011): 3-24. Oakes's presentation is unfortunately undermined by his overly selective choice of texts and the fact that his arguments all turn on making inaccurate claims of proof or authority, misrepresenting authors (including myself), or ignoring historico-critical contributions, the context of quotations, or theological distinctions. The editors declined to publish my analysis demonstrating these flaws.

the popes themselves have said about either Christ's descent into hell or about Balthasar. The authors simply characterize the case for his orthodoxy in fewer sentences than I did above, and then regard the matter as settled. Such brusqueness suggests the logic is self-evident and the conclusion necessary. The argument, however, turns on hasty assumptions about the approbation given Balthasar. Since a similarity in theologies might suggest a kind of approval, we will look at Balthasar's theology of the descent, then Ratzinger's (before and after his papal election), and finally that of Pope John Paul II. We will then see exactly what Benedict and John Paul II have said about Balthasar himself. I have attempted to consider here all the statements published to date (April, 2012) by Ratzinger/Benedict XVI and John Paul II on Christ's descent, as well as all those of the two popes on Balthasar. With such prolific authors, it is certainly possible I may have missed something. If so, I would ask the reader two things: First, take into account that any other texts do not change those examined here nor any clear conclusions that emerge from them. Second, do let me know!

1

BALTHASAR ON THE DESCENT

According to Balthasar, Christ's descent into hell is the pinnacle of the Trinity's self-revelation in salvation history. In this event, God's love remains unscathed by His descent into — and real union with — what is most not Himself, sin and the abandonment by God that is its punishment. The sovereign freedom necessary to punish sin and embrace this justice in love for the world's redemption will manifest God's trinitarian divinity.

Christ's Descent, Not His Cross, Completes the Redemption

Four specific details can help fill out this summary of Balthasar's theology of Christ's descent into hell (or *descensus*, which is Latin for *descent* and still sometimes used as a technical term to refer to this event). First, in Balthasar's view, the reconciliation of God with the world is not complete with Christ's death on the cross, but only with the Son's descent into hell. For, he says, "it is possible to distinguish between sin and the sinner."[1] He uses *distinguish* here in the sense of a real separation. Balthasar writes, "because of the energy that man has invested in it, sin is a reality, it is not 'nothing.'"[2] In other words, sin is not merely a defect in an action, or an

1. Hans Urs von Balthasar, *The Last Act*, vol. 5, *Theo-Drama*, trans. Graham Harrison (San Francisco: Ignatius, 1998), 266.

2. Balthasar, *Last Act*, 314. See also his *Mysterium Paschale: The Mystery of Easter*, trans. Aidan Nichols (Edinburgh: T. & T. Clark, 1990), 173; *Theology: The New Covenant*, vol. 7, *The Glory of the Lord: A Theological Aesthetics*, trans. Brian McNeil, ed. John Riches (San

action that lacks some good it ought to have; rather, sin has a kind of real being itself.[3] As such a reality, sin may be taken from the sinner and loaded upon another,[4] not just as a figure of speech or in idea, but in actuality. The transfer of sin to Christ begins in Gethsemane and is completed upon the cross.[5] Mankind is thus freed from the guilt of sin even before Christ's death. However, the separate reality of the sins themselves remains to be expiated. Balthasar insists that expiation occurs in the descent: Christ's death on the cross provides Him entrance to the state of being dead, which "constituted the term and aim of the Incarnation. . . . [For] only what has been endured is healed and saved."[6]

Christ's Suffering Increases in His Descent

Balthasar's principle that "only what has been endured is healed" resembles but significantly changes the patristic maxim, "What is not *assumed* is not healed." The Church Fathers were arguing that Christ was truly human, that the Son of God took upon Himself ("assumed") a whole human nature, both body and soul, and not a body only. In contrast, as we will shortly see confirmed, Balthasar's version concerns not nature, but punishment: Christ expiates ("heals") sin by undergoing ("enduring") the punishment for sin. Balthasar's principle is his premise for a second detail about his position: because Christ must bear all punishment for sin, His suffering intensifies after His death on the cross. "God has redeemed us," Balthasar reminds his reader, from "nothing less than hell, the eternal exclusion from the presence

---

Francisco: Ignatius, 1984), 233; and "Zur Frage: 'Hoffnung für alle' Eine Antwort auf den Artikel von Pfr. Karl Besler," *Theologisches* 199 (1986): 7365.

3. In contrast to St. Thomas Aquinas, e.g., *Summa Theologiae* Ia-IIae, q. 79, a. 2.

4. On the "load" of sin, see, e.g., Balthasar, *The New Covenant*, 208-9; and his *Leben aus dem Tod: Betrachtungen zum Ostermysterium* (Einsiedeln: Johannes, 1997), 36.

5. Balthasar, *Mysterium Paschale*, 101; *Leben aus dem Tod*, 36; and *The Action*, vol. 4, *Theo-Drama*, trans. Graham Harrison (San Francisco: Ignatius, 1994), 345.

6. Balthasar, *Mysterium Paschale*, 164-65. Balthasar inaccurately attributes the last sentence to St. Irenaeus. Most precisely, the term of the Incarnation is the "act of sharing" in the soul's descent "*ad infernum*" (Latin, "to hell") which Balthasar identifies with the state of "being dead" throughout the chapter. See also *Mysterium Paschale*, 150; "The Descent into Hell," *Spirit and Institution*, Explorations in Theology, vol. 4, trans. Edward T. Oakes (San Francisco: Ignatius, 1995), 411; and *New Covenant*, 395.

of God."[7] Our Savior is "conformed to his brethren even in this";[8] thus He descends "into ultimate perdition" and the "estrangement from God of hell" such that "he experiences the complete godlessness of lost man."[9]

Balthasar is explicit. "The interior death of sin . . . is the *terminus a quo* of the common Resurrection,"[10] that is, the extreme from which both Christ and sinners rise. Because physical death entered the world through the spiritual death that is sin (par. Rom 5:12), Balthasar thinks *both* spiritual death and physical death should be understood in texts such as Rom 14:9: "For to this end Christ died and lived again, that he might be Lord both of the dead and the living."[11] Thus the scars in Christ's risen body will reveal His "unique experience of death that is both spiritual and bodily."[12] "The reality of the *poena damni* [the pain of the loss of God in hell] is spiritual and can be experienced only spiritually."[13] Balthasar calls the pre-redeemed afterlife where Christ experiences spiritual death *Sheol.* (In my text here, I will capitalize *Sheol* wherever it is used in Balthasar's sense.) Parallel to St. Thomas Aquinas's statement that God unites Himself to the human intellect in the beatific vision,[14] Balthasar says,

> [Christ in Sheol] can and must be one with the object of his vision: the second death which, itself, is one with sheer sin as such, no longer sin as attaching to a particular human being . . . but abstracted from that individuation, contemplated in its bare reality as such.[15]

And as St. Thomas calls the beatific vision the *visio Dei* (the vision of God), Balthasar calls this infernal vision the *visio mortis* (the vision of death). This

7. Hans Urs von Balthasar, *The God Question and Modern Man*, trans. Hilda Graef (New York: Seabury, 1967), 133.

8. Balthasar, *God Question*, 133.

9. Hans Urs von Balthasar, "Trinity and Future," *Elucidations*, trans. John Riches (San Francisco: Ignatius, 1975), 82. See also Balthasar's *Mysterium Paschale*, 164-65, 167; *The New Covenant*, 225, 231-33; *God Question*, 132, 137; "Descent into Hell," 408; and "Some Points of Eschatology," in *The Word Made Flesh*, Explorations in Theology, vol. I, trans. A. V. Littledale and Alexander Dru (San Francisco: Ignatius, 1989), 264.

10. Balthasar, *Mysterium Paschale*, 155. See also Balthasar, *Leben aus dem Tod*, 50-51; and "Some Points of Eschatology," 264.

11. Balthasar, *Mysterium Paschale*, 155.

12. Balthasar, *Last Act*, 477.

13. Balthasar, *God Question*, 133.

14. Aquinas, *Summa Theologiae*, Ia q. 12, aa. 4, 9.

15. Balthasar, *Mysterium Paschale*, 173. Contrast Rev 20:14, which does not characterize "the second death" as Sheol.

passage and similar ones confirm that Balthasar's language of *separation, loading,* and the like are not merely metaphorical, as some claim. Instead, Balthasar treats sin as a real substance, one that always retains its essence of culpability deserving of punishment.

Christ Is Literally "Made Sin" and Consequently Undergoes the Father's Wrath

Because Christ alone experiences this intimate union with all sin, Balthasar stresses that Christ is "literally 'made sin' (2 Cor 5:21)"[16] in Sheol, which is a third facet of his theology. In the Incarnation, "the Son . . . 'lays up' and commits to God's keeping the 'form of God' he has received from him."[17] Just as Balthasar says the Son thus stripped Himself of divine attributes to be made man, so Christ will strip Himself of His being man to be made sin in Sheol:[18] "Holy Saturday is . . . a kind of suspension, as it were, of the Incarnation. . . ."[19] Lest one not take seriously this claim due to the "as it were," Balthasar elsewhere affirms "the removal of the whole superstructure of the Incarnation" that permits "the face-to-face confrontation between the 'naked' God and 'naked' sin."[20] It is not Christ (the *incarnate* Son of God), but just the Person of the Son, who undergoes the *visio mortis.* The reality of sin is intimately and spiritually united to His "naked" Person, denuded of both divine and human attributes. "Sheer sin as such" thus comes to exist in

16. Balthasar, *Leben aus dem Tod,* 36: "buchstäblich «zur Sünde gemacht» wird (2 Cor 5:21)."

17. Hans Urs von Balthasar, *The Dramatis Personae: The Person in Christ,* vol. III, *Theo-Drama,* trans. Graham Harrison (San Francisco: Ignatius, 1992), 228, with extended footnote.

18. Hans Urs von Balthasar, "Abstieg zur Hölle," *Pneuma und Institution,* bd. IV, *Skizzen zur Theologie* (Einsiedeln: Johannes, 1974), 397. See also the discussion in Alyssa Lyra Pitstick, *Light in Darkness: Hans Urs von Balthasar and the Catholic Doctrine of Christ's Descent into Hell* (Grand Rapids: Eerdmans, 2007), 148-58, 190-203; Balthasar, "Kenosis of the Church?" in *Spirit and Institution,* 138: "In the *kenosis* of the Son, it is true that his innate 'form of God' stays back with the Father, is 'left behind' with him . . ."; and Balthasar, *Church and World,* trans. A. V. Littledale with Alexander Dru (New York: Herder & Herder, 1967), 106-7, in which the Incarnation is stressed as "a real movement" by the reiteration of the Word's passing "from" the form of God "into" the form of man. Contrast Phil 2:6-7, which does not use the terminology *from* and *into*; indeed, the *kenosis* is not identified with the loss of divine attributes, but with the assumption of creaturely ones.

19. Balthasar, "Descent into Hell," 411-12.

20. Balthasar, *The New Covenant,* 231. See also Pitstick, *Light in Darkness,* 190-203.

His Person in the way His human nature had; in technical terms, it becomes enhypostasized in Him. There is "an *inner* appropriation of what is ungodly and hostile to God, an identification with that darkness of alienation from God into which the sinner falls as a result of his No."[21]

In virtue of this union, the Son will endure (and thus ultimately "heal") in His own Person (that is, as Son) the Father's wrath against sin and rejection of the sinner. Just as the Word's descent from heaven in the Incarnation ended with the death of the body, His descent to the state of being dead culminates with death, an archetypical spiritual death that is union with all sin and its punishment. This punishment is complete abandonment by the Father. Since the one who undergoes it in this case is the one who lived from and for Him, the Son suffers the Father's abandonment in proportion to the original love and closeness between them. Thus, the Son's experience of Sheol is infinitely *worse* than anything we could call hell: the divine Son suffers union with the anti-divine reality of sin; He suffers the Father's wrath and rejection due to this union; and He suffers that abandonment inasmuch as He is Son and in His very relation to the Father.

Sin Is Expiated within the Trinity

How does this event complete redemption? By bringing the sins of mankind into the being of the Son, they are simultaneously brought into the Trinity, where even as the Father unleashes His wrath against sin onto the Son, the Holy Spirit will unite both of them in the divine love.[22] In this way, the divine love will prove itself greater than all sin, thereby rendering sins ultimately powerless to separate men from God.[23] This way of expiating sin highlights the fourth characteristic of Balthasar's theology of Holy Saturday: besides being the climax of redemption and the peak of the Son's suffering in His literally being made sin, the descent is a trinitarian event in that all three Persons experience it, albeit in different ways.[24] The Son suffers the Father's abandonment, wrath, and rejection; the Father suffers the loss of

21. Balthasar, *Action*, 334, emphasis in original. See also Balthasar, "Loneliness in the Church," *Spirit and Institution*, 269.

22. See, e.g., Balthasar, *Last Act*, 262; and "Scapegoat and the Trinity," *You Crown the Year with Your Goodness*, trans. Graham Harrison (San Francisco: Ignatius, 1989), 85.

23. See Balthasar, "On Vicarious Representation," *Spirit and Institution*, 421; "Death Is Swallowed Up by Life," *Communio ICR* 14, no. 2 (1987): 50-51.

24. See, e.g., Balthasar, *Action*, 501.

the Son and His own wrath; and the Spirit connects Father and Son in their reciprocal abandonment.

* * *

The reader will get a sense of how Balthasar's theology compares to Catholic doctrine on Christ's descent into hell when the two universal catechisms of the Catholic Church (the *Roman Catechism* and the *Catechism of the Catholic Church*) are discussed in Chapter 4. (Extensive textual references and a more detailed presentation of Balthasar's ideas and comparison with Catholic doctrine may be found in *Light in Darkness*.) The catechisms' sections on Christ's descent are also reproduced in their entirety in the appendices.

2

RATZINGER ON THE DESCENT

Although Balthasar sees the infinitude of divine love as the foundation of his descent theology, that love takes concrete form in the Son's horrific union with the *visio mortis*, conformity to all sin in His very being, and consequent God-abandonment and experience of the divine wrath. Before his papal election, the approach in some of Ratzinger's best-known works is similar to Balthasar's in that he too proposes a descent to suffering, but he moves away from the extremity of his friend's descriptions in favor of a psychological experience prior to death. In other places, however, Ratzinger portrays the descent as an event in which Christ brings His own communion into a human condition of ultimate loneliness.

Introduction to Christianity (1968)

In what is perhaps his most widely read book, *Introduction to Christianity*, Ratzinger opens his brief treatment of the descent by noting that although there is a certain primacy of the word, because God is Word, God's revelation includes His times of silence:[1]

1. Joseph Ratzinger, *Einführung in das Christentum: Vorlesungen über das Apostolische Glaubensbekenntnis* (Munich: Kösel, 2000), 278-79. This text was originally published in 1968.

> Only if we have experienced Him as silent may we hope also to hear His speech, which proceeds in silence. Christology reaches out past the cross, the moment of the tangibility of God's love, into death, into the silence and the obscuring [*Verdunklung*] of God. Can we wonder that the Church, that the life of the individual, is ever again led into this hour of silence, into the forgotten and shoved aside article, "descended into hell"?[2]

The article's meaning is illuminated, Ratzinger says, by Christ's words from the cross, "My God, My God, why have You abandoned Me?" Ratzinger insists it is important to recall that exactly these words open Psalm 22, that prayer in a situation of desperate need that nevertheless ends in hope. The psalm on the lips of Christ suggests a model for the worship of Christians in their own trials:

> Can it be anything other than the cry from the deep together with the Lord, who "descended into hell," and established the nearness of God in the middle of abandonment by God?[3]

Although this reference to abandonment seems to echo Balthasar, shortly before this question Ratzinger had used a quote from Ernst Käsemann to highlight how Christ's committed cry for the Father contrasts with everything earthly that says God is absent.[4] Here the descent, such as it is, happens *on this side of death*: it is the experience of the temptation to give up on God when we do not "see" Him and He is "silent." Moreover, God's abandonment is *only apparent*; it is not real, as it was in Balthasar's theology.

2. Ratzinger, *Einführung*, 279.

3. Ratzinger, *Einführung*, 280.

4. Ratzinger, *Einführung*, 279-80. Ratzinger will again underscore that the Father's absence is only apparent in his meditation on Good Friday in *Dogma und Verkundigung* (Munich: Erich Wewel, 1973), published in English as *Dogma and Preaching*, trans. Matthew J. O'Connell (Chicago: Franciscan Herald, 1985). Ratzinger highlights first that Jesus' cry is a prayer; by directing His cry to God, Jesus affirms the Father is there, despite appearances (35). Second, Ratzinger points out that "the claim that there can no longer be any God . . . is the urgent conclusion drawn by *onlookers* at the terror. . . . But among those who are themselves immersed in the fearful reality the effect is not infrequently just the opposite: It is precisely then that they discover God" (35, emphasis in original). Consequently, in such situations where God appears absent, God is also to be found in these least of our brethren: they know that "in Christ God suffered with them" and that they are "identified with the crucified Christ" in their own sufferings and "thereby drawn into the abyss of everlasting mercy" (36-37). The cross is a horror rejected by mere onlookers, but the instrument of redemption to those united to Christ.

Ratzinger goes on to approach the question from another, complementary angle. He again says the cry from the cross expressed the central meaning of Jesus's descent, but this time he identifies the descent's significance as Christ's "sharing in the human fate of death."[5] The deepest element of His passion was not physical pain, but radical loneliness.[6] On the one hand, this loneliness is that of the human person in his most profound interior, to which no other human has full access.[7] On the other, "there is a door, through which we can only step alone, the door of death. All the fear of the world is, in the end, the fear of this loneliness."[8] Loneliness and death are connected because death severs all communion as we know it.[9] Such loneliness in both senses would become hell as theology names it, he says, when it is so total that no word, no hand, can reach into it.[10] For Ratzinger, the creedal article on the descent means that "Christ has stepped through the door of our ultimate loneliness, that He in His passion has entered into this abyss of our abandonment."[11]

This phrase again sounds like Balthasar, but Ratzinger does not explicitly extend Christ's abandonment beyond the threshold of death, for he goes on to say, "Where no more voice can reach, He is there. *With that* is hell overthrown, or more precisely, the *death* that was hell before is no more. Neither death nor hell is the same, because in the middle of death stands Life and dwells Love."[12] Christ's entrance as love into that loneliness is its overthrow. Although Balthasar uses similar language and asserts that Love suffers on the other side of the door, Ratzinger could be locating all suffering on this side, in Christ's human fear of death, while on the other side, and even in the event of death itself, He brings communion into what humans fear will be loneliness.

Eschatology (1977)

Or maybe not. In his famous *Eschatology*, Ratzinger seems to be explicit when he says, "The true Bodhisattva, Christ, goes into hell and suffers it

5. Ratzinger, *Einführung*, 280.
6. Ratzinger, *Einführung*, 280.
7. Ratzinger, *Einführung*, 280.
8. Ratzinger, *Einführung*, 283.
9. Ratzinger, *Einführung*, 280-83.
10. Ratzinger, *Einführung*, 282.
11. Ratzinger, *Einführung*, 283.
12. Ratzinger, *Einführung*, 283, emphasis added.

empty."[13] Again with strong echoes of Balthasar, Ratzinger speaks of the "darkness of Jesus' descent to Sheol," the "suffered-through night of His soul," "the darkness of His descent into the night," "the freedom of His love that goes into the Abyss," and the likeness of some of the mystics to Christ in their willingness "to leave their salvation behind for the sake of others."[14]

Because Ratzinger does not identify the reality to which the metaphorical language of "darkness" and "night" point, however, one ought not just assume he is affirming Balthasar's theses. The texts themselves do not provide enough information to support that conclusion. Indeed, in speaking of the "night of His *soul*," Ratzinger specifies that Christ suffered in His humanity, not His divinity. He thus takes a position different from Balthasar's, who is explicit that the Son suffers in His *divine* relation to the Father.

Does Christ suffer this "night of the soul" before or after His death? Ratzinger's text is not sufficiently explicit to say. Given what Ratzinger had said about human loneliness and the temptation to despair in his *Introduction to Christianity*, the characterization of Christ as the Bodhisattva who "goes into hell" and shares human suffering can as truly refer to pre-death psychological "hells" as to some abode of the afterlife, just as the appeal to the mystics' "dark night of faith"[15] is insufficient to establish anything more than some experience by Christ of the *seeming* absence of God during this life. St. John of the Cross, St. Theresa of Avila, and the other masters of the spiritual life insist that experience of abandonment by God, when not the separation we inflict on ourselves through mortal sin, is quite opposite one's feeling: God is drawing closer. The analogy is the person blinded not by darkness, but by light beyond the eyes' capacity.

Similarly, "the love that goes into the Abyss" could as truly describe God's unchanging love of His creatures, even if they are damned, or Christ's bringing His communion to human loneliness, as it is could a Balthasarian *visio mortis* by the Son.

13. Joseph Ratzinger, *Eschatologie: Tod und ewiges Leben*, vol. 9 of Johann Auer and Joseph Ratzinger, *Kleine Katholische Dogmatik* (Regensburg: Pustet, 1977), 177. Although there are variations among the different forms of Buddhism, in general terms a *bodhisattva* is a being who has essentially achieved enlightenment but who turns back to the suffering world to help all those there likewise reach enlightenment.

14. Ratzinger, *Eschatologie*, 178.

15. Ratzinger, *Eschatologie*, 178.

Whether Ratzinger *meant* something as strong as Balthasar, he did not actually *say* it, so the burden of proof is on anyone who would make that claim. For the sake of the argument, I would be willing to grant he did.

"Meditations on Holy Week," Introduction (1997)

I would, except that we will then entangle Ratzinger in a self-contradiction. At the time that he was preparing his lectures for his 1967 summer course *Introduction to Christianity*, he also wrote five "Meditations on Holy Week" for Bavarian Radio. These have been republished in a book of William G. Congdon's paintings, *The Sabbath of History*, for which Ratzinger wrote a special introduction in 1997. In reflecting on his personal outlook at the time he wrote the meditations, Ratzinger says,

> I was asked in the summer of 1956 to review a new book of Hans Urs von Balthasar (*Die Gottesfrage des heutigen Menschen*, Vienna: Herder, 1956) in which the author shifts the article on the descent into hell to the center of Christian faith and life. According to Balthasar, Christ participated himself in hell, in the deepest sense of the word; only in the last level of his descent did redemption penetrate into the deepest abyss, that is to say, hell. At the time I did not want to adopt this thesis. . . . I have to admit that even today [that is, in 1997], as in 1956 and 1967, I find it difficult fully to concur with the great Swiss theologian with whom I developed a close friendship. I prefer to leave this mysterious sentence, which leads from the historical world into the hiddenness of death, in its mysterious obscurity.[16]

It seems unlikely, then, that Ratzinger meant his 1977 *Eschatology* to be understood in a strictly Balthasarian sense, given that before and after 1977, he did not agree with Balthasar's theses, at least not wholly. Unfortunately, Ratzinger does not specify the exact nature or extent of his difficulties.

He goes on to say, however, that he thought then, and still thought in 1997, that a way forward might be to consider the suggestion of some

16. Joseph Ratzinger, "Five Meditations," *The Sabbath of History* (Washington, DC: William G. Congdon Foundation, 2000), 21. The introduction is dated 1997; the book's publication date is 2000. *Die Gottesfrage* was published in English as *The God Question and Modern Man*, trans. Hilda Graef (New York: Seabury, 1967).

exegetes that, since *sheol* is merely the Hebrew word for the realm of the dead, saying Christ descended into it might be equivalent to saying He died.[17] But that of course only raises other questions, such as, What is death?[18]

Two points are worth digression here. First, among those other questions raised, Ratzinger does not ask an important one: before the descent clause the creed explicitly states that Christ died, so why should it have such duplication? Already ca. AD 404, Rufinus's commentary on the creed suggested an answer: because the descent article's purpose is *not* the mere assertion of death. Instead, it affirms a distinct event, one with its own significance. Hence Rufinus provides separate scriptural support for burial and descent, ultimately characterizing the descent with the analogy of a king personally setting free his servants from a conquered prison.[19] Not only is Rufinus's commentary valuable for illustrating that the doctrine's significance was well developed early in Church history, his analogy neatly captures the traditional Christian doctrine, about which we will see more when we look at John Paul II's theology.

The second point that Ratzinger overlooks is that the creeds with a descent clause are originally in Latin and they do *not* say Christ "descended into sheol"; they say He descended to "those below" [Latin variants *ad inferos, ad infernos, ad inferna*]. It is not the creeds, but the common Christian heritage of Sacred Tradition that specifies this expression to mean the descent of Christ's soul to sheol (or, in Greek, to *hades*). Although the belief was almost certainly first expressed using the Greek term, or possibly the Hebrew one (because the Church spread from the East), it was first explicitly codified in Latin creeds. Whatever the exact way in which the article entered the creed, without doubt it is Sacred Tradition that maintains the equivalency among the terms in the three languages afterward. But that is not all.

We must keep in mind that, without revelation, we do not know what the afterlife is like: the bereft living hesitate to characterize it as perfect happiness, since the rejoicing that would then be appropriate violates their emotions. Yet thinking it is loneliness and abandonment (as Ratzinger describes

17. Ratzinger, "Five Meditations," 21-22.

18. Ratzinger, "Five Meditations," 22.

19. Rufinus, *A Commentary on the Apostles' Creed*, trans. W. H. Fremantle, Nicene and Post-Nicene Fathers, 2nd ser., vol. 3 (Grand Rapids: Eerdmans, 1979), #17, 27-28, 55, 60-61. See Alois Grillmeier, "Der Gottessohn im Totenreich: Soteriologische und christologische Motivierung der Descensuslehre in der älteren christlichen Überlieferung," *Mit ihm und in ihm: Christologische Forschungen und Perspektiven*, 2. Auflage (Freiburg: Herder, 1975), 76-174, on the early awareness of the descent's soteriological significance.

it, for example) may be equally a projection of the survivors' sentiments. On our own, we just do not know. Even after-death experiences can offer, at best, a short glimpse beyond the door, one that cannot bear the weight of a claim to be definitive. So Ratzinger is right to hesitate to speak of the afterlife insofar as unaided reason is substantially ignorant of it.

However, just as knowledge of the Trinity depends on revelation, God may reveal something true of death and what lies beyond — and for Catholic theologians, God's revelation includes Sacred Tradition. (Put differently in part, one thing Tradition does is clarify the meaning of God's revelation in Scripture.) That Tradition has not been silent about the character of the abode where Christ descended, nor about what occurred there: the same Tradition that specifies that Christ descended to sheol insists that sheol/hades is not to be characterized by the Old Testament alone, but also by Christ (for example, in His parable of Lazarus and His promise to the good thief); that He did not suffer in His descent; and that He was triumphant in the ordinary sense of the word.

Why Ratzinger accepts the Tradition's specification of "those below" as sheol and does not likewise integrate the other elements is unknown.

Let us return to Ratzinger puzzling to himself about just this question, What is death? He says, "At the same time the solution to the questions occurred" to him.[20] He then goes on to say something that also appears almost verbatim in *Introduction to Christianity*:

> Yes, Jesus died, he "descended" into the mysterious depths death leads to. He went to the ultimate solitude where no one can accompany us, for "being dead" is above all loss of communication. It is isolation where love does not penetrate. In this sense Christ descended "into hell" whose essence is precisely the loss of love, being cut off from God and man. But, however, *wherever he goes, "hell" ceases to be hell, because he himself is life and love,* because he is the bridge which connects man and God and thereby also connects men among themselves. And thus the descent is *at the same time* also transformation. The final solitude no longer exists — except for the one who wants it, who rejects love from within and from its foundation, because he seeks only himself, wants to be from and for himself.[21]

20. Ratzinger, "Five Meditations," 22.
21. Ratzinger, "Five Meditations," 22, emphasis added.

Here again, despite similarities to Balthasar in the language of "ultimate solitude" and "hell" as "being cut off from God and man," there are significant conceptual differences. For Ratzinger, the Incarnation remains intact. Christ is Himself inalienably "the bridge which connects man and God": in remaining irrevocably united to His own human nature, the Son of God is thereby also united to all others of the human race as their brother. Similarly, as God incarnate, Christ brings with Him into the abode of the dead "life and love" and apparently these as commonly understood, not as Balthasar has the Spirit bridging alienation unbeknownst to the Son in Sheol. As Ratzinger will say in ***God Is Near Us*** **(2001)**, just a couple years after his introduction to "Meditations,"

> For all the differences there may be between the accounts in the various Gospels, there is one point in common: Jesus died praying, and in the abyss of death he upheld the First Commandment and held on to the presence of God.[22]

In his introduction to "Meditations," Ratzinger locates Christ's descent after death, while in his *Introduction to Christianity* it is identified with Christ's approach to death; what remains consistent between the two, however, supports a non-Balthasarian reading of the *Introduction*. Namely, because of who He is, Christ's very entrance overthrows hell, not only for Himself, but for all who, like Him, are intimately united with God. He does not dwell there for a time, experiencing that loneliness Himself; rather His entrance into what — without Him — is loneliness, shatters it for those united with Him. As Ratzinger had said earlier, in **"Taking Bearings in Christology" (1982)**,

> The last words of Jesus were an expression of his devotion to his Father. . . . His dying was itself an act of prayer, his death was a handing-over of himself to the Father. . . . Death, which, by its very nature, is the end, the destruction of every communication, is changed by him into an

22. Joseph Ratzinger, *God Is Near Us: The Eucharist, the Heart of Life* (San Francisco: Ignatius, 2003), 39. The German original had been published two years earlier: *Gott ist uns nah. Eucharistie: Mitte des Lebens* (Augsburg: Sankt Ulrich, 2001). Ratzinger footnotes this passage, "This reflection was adumbrated by E. Käsemann in 1967, in an address at the Congress of the German Evangelical Church (published under the title: 'Die Gegenwart des Gekreuzigten' [The Presence of the Crucified], in E. Käsemann, *Kirchliche Konflikte*, vol. I [Göttingen, 1982], pp. 76-91, especially 77, 80f.)."

> act of self-communication; and this is man's redemption, for it signifies the triumph of love over death.[23]

Christ's self-gift to the Father at the moment of His death changes death from isolation to passage to perfect communion.

The Spirit of the Liturgy (2000)

Although this communion is perfected for us above all through union with the Persons of the Trinity, it should be noted that for those with mortal nature it must also entail the definitive overcoming of death's dissolution of the body-soul unity. Hence Ratzinger will later say, in *God Is Near Us* (2001), that it is "by the Resurrection [that] God accepts this death [of Christ] and makes it the door into a new life."[24] He made the same point in *The Spirit of the Liturgy* (2000), using a biblical analogy:

> For Christians, the Resurrection of Christ is the true Exodus. He has stridden through the Red Sea of death itself, descended into the world of shadows, and smashed open the prison door. In Baptism this Exodus is made ever present. To be baptized is to be made a partaker, a contemporary, of Christ's descent into hell and of his rising up therefrom, in which he takes us up into the fellowship of new life.[25]

Here, set apart from Christ's death though made possible by it, His descent and resurrection are linked as that by which definitive life is communicated to those united to Him.

23. Joseph Ratzinger, "Taking Bearings in Christology," *Behold the Pierced One*, trans. Graham Harrison (San Francisco: Ignatius, 1986), 24-25. This address was originally given in 1982 and published in the original German anthology *Schauen auf den Durchbohrten* (Einsiedeln: Johannes, 1984). This "transformation of death into an act of love" is the key, Ratzinger says, to understanding Christ's death as His glorification ("Taking Bearings," 24).

24. Ratzinger, *God Is Near Us*, 39.

25. Joseph Ratzinger, *The Spirit of the Liturgy* (San Francisco: Ignatius, 2000), 137-38. The German original (*Der Geist der Liturgie. Eine Einführung*) was published the same year by Herder (Freiburg).

"Meditations on Holy Week" (1967)

Ratzinger's 1997 introductory remarks to his "Meditations on Holy Week" are worth bearing in mind as one considers the five meditations themselves, the last three of which concern Holy Saturday. The first of these three draws an analogy between two pairs: on the one hand, there is the "death of God" theology then current and the reduction of one's faith life to rote and mediocrity; on the other hand, there is the silence and emptiness felt by the disciples after the burial of Christ. This meditation is associated with the descent in its reference to "Holy Saturday, the day of the burial of God"[26] and to *Christians'* (not Christ's) consequent sense of God's absence on that day, similar to the disciples' dreariness as they left the cross or walked to Emmaus. This first meditation nonetheless does not pronounce on the nature of Christ's descent itself.

The second meditation does, at least in part. Ratzinger first says, "No one can really explain"[27] Christ's descent. Ratzinger pursues his way forward based on his speculation about the nature of death as loneliness, an approach retained in *Introduction to Christianity* as we have already seen: the creedal profession "means that Christ has traversed the gate of loneliness, that he has descended into the unreachable, insurmountable ground of abandonment" — so much sounds like Balthasar, but then —

> It means that even in the last night in which no word can be heard . . . there is a voice that calls us, a hand that takes and leads us. The insuperable loneliness of man is overcome since *He* was there in it. Hell is overcome since love has also entered into the region of death. . . . Since there has been the presence of love in the realm of death, there is life in the midst of death.[28]

For Ratzinger here, this loneliness is not Balthasar's intratrinitarian God-abandonment, but *our* lack of perfect communion with God. It is not clear, however, whether this loneliness is just what death is, or if the experience is somehow connected with personal sin in a way that would make it also punishment for us. Then again, Christ's loneliness may simply be the human condition in the face of death after the Fall. For Ratzinger continues,

26. Ratzinger, "Five Meditations," 38.
27. Ratzinger, "Five Meditations," 42.
28. Ratzinger, "Five Meditations," 45, emphasis in original.

> No one can imagine what the words "descended into hell" mean in the end. But when we ourselves approach the hour of our final solitude, we will be permitted to grasp something of this dark mystery. We can now only have some presentiment of the trusting certainty that we shall not be alone in that hour of deepest forsakenness.[29]

It seems, then, that Christ overcomes the loneliness both of our fear of approaching death and of isolation in death by establishing in them the communion of His love.

Noting Ratzinger's protestations of ignorance regarding this mystery, we observe again the ambiguity in his speculation. Does he mean Christ's descent can give us comfort in our loneliest living hours, including when we approach our final hour? Surely so much, but also surely that would not exhaust the descent's significance. Does he mean there is some comfort to be had also in hell itself, even when *hell* is understood not only as "the region of death," but as the realm of eternal punishment? That is not entirely ruled out. Did Christ suffer loneliness after death and if so, what did it mean for Him? Ratzinger does not say; if anything, he seems again to suggest Christ did not suffer such loneliness, for, as the Word Incarnate, He brought the presence of God in His own Person into that loneliness, thereby changing it into a way of communion. Christ goes where we would be definitively lonely, but because of who He is, He is not lonely there.

Ratzinger's final meditation, which is also the last of the three on Holy Saturday, ends his reflections in a way that confirms this conclusion. First, taking the Divine Office of the breviary as his point of departure, he says,

> If one tries to summarize the liturgical prayer of Holy Saturday, one will be touched above all by the deep peace it breathes. Christ has entered into concealment, but also amid impenetrable dark *into safety*, indeed, he has become the last security of us all.[30]

His presence in the abyss of death ratifies in the fullest sense possible the psalmist's confidence in God that "if I make my bed in sheol, thou art there."[31]

29. Ratzinger, "Five Meditations," 46. Compare Grillmeier, who closes "Gottessohn im Totenreich," 174, by alluding to how the Word's descent into death by means of His human nature is a descent into the greatest depth of our existence.

30. Ratzinger, "Five Meditations," 47, emphasis added.

31. Psalm 139:8, as quoted by Ratzinger, "Five Meditations," 47.

Ratzinger continues by describing Holy Saturday as already sharing in the glory of Easter:

> Thus this liturgy proceeds like the sunrise, the first light of Easter morning shines into it. If Good Friday places before our eyes the buffeted figure of the pierced one, Holy Saturday's liturgy is as much reminiscent of the early Church's view of the cross, surrounded by beams of light, as much symbol of resurrection as of death [sic].[32]

This perspective constitutes another difference between Ratzinger and Balthasar. For the *Anastasis* icons of the Christian East, which show Christ in glory after His death drawing Adam, Eve, and other holy people to Himself out of their graves, similarly connect Christ's descent and resurrection, and these Balthasar abhors. In his view,

> [They manifest a] theological busyness and religious impatience which insist on anticipating the moment of fruiting of the eternal redemption through the temporal passion — on dragging forward that moment from Easter to Holy Saturday.[33]

The second focus of Ratzinger's last meditation is eschatological. Here he ties this light of Easter, already seen in Holy Saturday, to Good Friday, with which his "Meditations for Holy Week" opened. Reviving an ancient dimension of Christian piety, he refers to the cross as the standard borne before the coming King. In this image of the King, the King is present in the midst of the community He has drawn to Himself, even as they await His definitive coming. Christ's sovereign standard of the cross is connected also to the direction of the East:

> The Christians prayed turned toward the East as a sign of their hope that Christ, the true sun, would rise over history. . . . Thus for early Christendom the cross is above all a sign of hope, not so much a turning toward the past as a turning toward the coming Lord.[34]

32. Ratzinger, "Five Meditations," 47.

33. Hans Urs von Balthasar, *Mysterium Paschale: The Mystery of Easter*, trans. Aidan Nichols (Edinburgh: T. & T. Clark, 1990), 179.

34. Ratzinger, "Five Meditations," 48.

Thus the unity of the past events wrought in Christ with their future completion as He has promised, in which the present Christian believes, is in some way encapsulated in the liturgy of Holy Saturday:

> But have we not then virtually forgotten . . . the unity of past and future in the Christian? The spirit of hope which the prayers of Holy Saturday breathe should permeate our entire Christian existence. Christianity is not merely a religion of the past, but equally of the future.[35]

Ratzinger closes his "Meditations" with a prayer: "Lord Jesus Christ, in the darkness of death you have brought light; in the abyss of the deepest loneliness abides now and always the powerful protection of your love."[36] As Ratzinger says in *Introduction to Christianity*, "Dying is a path into icy loneliness no more; the gates of Sheol are opened."[37]

Behold the Pierced One: "The Passover of Jesus and the Church" (1981), "The Lamb Redeemed the Sheep" (1984), "Christ the Liberator" (1984)

Our final texts by Ratzinger before his election as pope are "Three Meditations" in the anthology, *Behold the Pierced One*. They are brief, and the exposition here can be likewise, though some additional attention must be given to the third meditation. These meditations again connect Holy Saturday with Easter. However, in effect, they largely use the descent as a placeholder for the resurrection, apparently because the descent issues in the resurrection. What happened in the descent itself, and its own importance, remain unaddressed.

The first meditation is "The Passover of Jesus and the Church," a sermon for Holy Thursday delivered in 1981 and originally published in German with the other meditations in 1984. The descent is identified with Christ's free engagement with the fearfulness of death, in which His power and victory are already manifest.

> [After the Passover meal, Jesus] went out into the night. He did not fear the chaos, did not hide from it, but plunged into its deepest point,

35. Ratzinger, "Five Meditations," 49.
36. Ratzinger, "Five Meditations," 51.
37. Ratzinger, *Einführung*, 283.

> into the jaws of death: as we pray, he "descended into hell." . . . Faith always means going out together with Jesus, not being afraid of the chaos, because he is the stronger one. . . . He went out into the night of Gethsemane, the night of the Cross and the grave.[38]

— The descent is entrance "into the jaws of death," "the night of the Cross and the grave"; what lies beyond is not specified, except that, as seen before, they are transformed by Christ's presence —

> He is the "stronger man" who stands up against the "strong man" — death — (Lk 11:21-23). The love of God — God's power — is stronger than the powers of destruction. So this very "going out", this setting out on the path of the Passion, when Jesus steps outside the boundary of the protective walls of the city, is a gesture of victory. The mystery of Gethsemane already holds within it the mystery of Easter joy. Jesus is the "stronger man". There is no power that can withstand him now; no place where he is not to be found. He summons us to dare to accompany him on his path; for where faith and love are, he is there, and the power of peace is there which overcomes nothingness and death.[39]

The victory contained within this resoluteness of Christ will have an echo in *Jesus of Nazareth*, where Ratzinger will characterize Christ's obedience in Gethsemane as His high priestly sacrifice, as we will see in the next chapter.

Ratzinger's second meditation in *Behold the Pierced One*, "The Lamb Redeemed the Sheep," is an exquisitely structured reflection on how Christ as the sacrificed and risen paschal Lamb manifests God's provident love to us. This revelation of God "opens heaven" to us in showing us the truth of God.[40] Since Ratzinger sets the context for his discussion of the sacrificed Lamb by opening his meditation with Christ's descent, it is worth noting that historically the "opening of heaven" was a phrase used especially to refer to the union with God that Christ brought about for the souls of the holy dead during His descent. Ratzinger's language is consequently provocative, because with a phrase typically used in such a context for the perfect seeing of God in the next life, he refers to a revelation only ever partially understood in this life.

38. Ratzinger, "The Passover of Jesus and the Church: A Meditation for Holy Thursday," *Behold the Pierced One*, 108-9.

39. Ratzinger, "Passover of Jesus," 109.

40. See this theme throughout Ratzinger, "'The Lamb Redeemed the Sheep': Reflections on the Symbolism of Easter," *Behold the Pierced One*, for example, 177, 120.

Before his discussion of the Lamb, however, Ratzinger sets up his explicit reference to the descent with an acknowledgement that "we are only acquainted with things on this side of death."[41] Even so-called after-death experiences are not conclusive, because their temporary character suggests they are not definitive.[42] In such a context, Christ's resurrection becomes particularly important:

> But he of whom Easter speaks — Jesus Christ — really "descended into hell". Jesus actually complied with the suggestion of the rich man: Let someone come back from the dead, and we will believe (Lk 16:27f.)! He, the true Lazarus, *did* come back so that we may believe. And do we? He did not come back with disclosures nor with exciting prospects of the "world beyond." But he did tell us that he is "going to prepare a place" for us (Jn 14:2-3).[43]

Ratzinger's point is that, as the definitive Lazarus, Christ's descent *into* death is significant because it means Christ rose *from* death. The descent is again essentially identified with death. As the consequence of death, the descent is certainly to be associated with it, but one must ask if a simple identification of the two exhausts the descent's meaning. For something of significance might have occurred in the descent itself, which is implicit in Christ's "going to prepare a place": though His promise to do so is mentioned by Ratzinger here in a context after Christ's resurrection, the gospel places it as occurring before His death. Thus His "going" would include His descent, but Ratzinger does not elaborate how the descent figures in that preparation.

In Ratzinger's third meditation, "Christ the Liberator," the descent is similarly significant because it means Christ rises from death and so He is not bound by it. Thus when Ratzinger refers to the descent, he immediately goes on to expand upon the resurrection. The descent appears to have been collapsed into the resurrection, with the consequence that any additional importance of the descent in its own right is unaddressed.

Ratzinger opens with the Eastern Church's *Anastasis* icon. It is, he says, a "picture of Easter."[44]

41. Ratzinger, "Lamb Redeemed the Sheep," 111.
42. Ratzinger, "Lamb Redeemed the Sheep," 112.
43. Ratzinger, "Lamb Redeemed the Sheep," 112, emphasis in original.
44. Ratzinger, "Christ the Liberator: An Easter Homily," *Behold the Pierced One*, 123.

> [It] represents as it were the mysterious inner dimension of the event of Easter which . . . we profess in the Creed when we say, "He descended into hell". In the perspective of the icon, this is an affirmation concerning Jesus' victory. It depicts him as the "stronger man" who has opened and penetrated the domain of the "strong man". It portrays him as the Victor, having burst through the supposedly impregnable fortress of death, such that death is now no longer a place of no return; its doors lie open. Christ, in the aura of his wounded love, stands in this doorway, addresses the still somnolent Adam and takes him by the hand to lead him forth. The liturgy of Holy Saturday circles around this event.[45]

Tensions between descent and resurrection shadow this passage. The descent is, Ratzinger says, an Easter event, indeed the one that centers Holy Saturday's liturgy, including the Easter Vigil. However, the descent as part of Jesus's victory is qualified as "the perspective of the icon." Is that understanding then limited to the realm of artistic expression? Yet the doctrinal significance of icons was affirmed both by the blood of those martyred in the iconoclastic controversies and by the Fourth Ecumenical Council of Constantinople, which decreed that icons are to be given the same veneration as the book of Gospels.[46] If the Church's icons transmit in images the revelation that Scripture conveys through words, then the fact that the icons portray Christ's descent as a victorious event and part of Christ's Easter triumph is not merely an individual or peculiar perspective but an expression of the faith of the Church.

The ambiguity about whether the descent itself is part of Christ's victory is mirrored in the ambiguity of the timing Ratzinger describes: "having burst" the doors of death so that it is "no longer a place of no return" sounds like Christ's resurrection, but addressing "the still somnolent Adam" sounds like an encounter of Christ in the realm of the dead or possibly at the end of time. Although Christ's descent, His resurrection, and the final resurrection may all be represented by this multivalent icon,[47] those events are not simultaneous. Hence Ratzinger's mixed signals about time leave the reader unclear about which event he has in mind.

45. Ratzinger, "Christ the Liberator," 123. Ratzinger footnotes the last sentence, "Cf. the convincing remarks of P. Evdokimov, *L'Art de l'icône. Théologie de la beauté* (Desclée 1970), 265-75."

46. Jacques Dupuis, ed., *The Christian Faith in the Doctrinal Documents of the Catholic Church*, 6th ed. (Staten Island, NY: Alba House, 1996), #1253 (DS 653-54).

47. See Alyssa Lyra Pitstick, *Light in Darkness: Hans Urs von Balthasar and the Catholic Doctrine of Christ's Descent into Hell* (Grand Rapids: Eerdmans, 2007), 77.

An important question about the descent's significance also surfaces from the characterization of Christ in His descent as the "stronger man," an echo of Ratzinger's Holy Thursday meditation. Both meditations identify the "strong man" as death. In its Scriptural context, however, in which Christ is said to cast out demons by the power of Beelzebul, the "strong man" is not death personified, but Satan. (In the Holy Thursday meditation, Ratzinger referenced Lk 11:21-23, the Lucan verses on the strong man; the antecedent is provided by Lk 11:14-20 and echoed in the parallels in Matthew and Mark.) While death is connected with the domain of the devil for a variety of reasons, death is really a secondary enemy of humanity, because it is an *effect* of demonic and human sin, as the story of the Fall teaches (Gen 3; see also Wis 2:24: "through the devil's envy death entered the world"). Hence by jumping to interpret the strong man in this derivative sense of death, Ratzinger again leaves the reader wondering whether the descent might not have a fuller significance than simply being the necessary precursor to Christ's bodily resurrection.

Ratzinger moves on from the icon to consider part of the ancient homily ascribed to Epiphanius used in the Liturgy of the Hours for the day. The homily portrays Christ descending to the souls of the holy dead and speaking in particular to Adam. Ratzinger takes a phrase of the thrilling discourse ascribed to Christ as foundation for the rest of his meditation: "I did not make you for the dungeon." Ratzinger then immediately says that "this Adam does not signify an individual in a dim and distant past: the Adam addressed by the victorious Christ is we ourselves" and "this prison which Christ opens" is not the netherworld, but "the prisons of this world," including the prison of seeming freedom amid riches.[48]

The descent and resurrection have been collapsed here. For one, if Adam is the living and Christ is to lead us out of our prisons, that happens in virtue of the historical resurrection, the announcement of the good news that follows, and one's grasping His hand by faith in this life. What then happened in the afterlife to our first parents, to the dead patriarchs and prophets, to Christ, during the time His body lay in the tomb? That is the question of the descent, not of Easter, and one Ratzinger does not answer despite his use of the icon and the homily that references it.

After all, the homilist is talking about Christ's descent, even if Ratzinger repeatedly refers what he says to Easter. The descent may indeed be an "Easter event," as Ratzinger has said, but that does not mean they are

48. Ratzinger, "Christ the Liberator," 124.

identical. Certainly it makes sense that what Christ is represented to say to Adam in the homily is meant also for the homily's hearers, and so it also makes sense to take the prison of the netherworld as an analogue for prisons, real and metaphorical, in this life. What is odd is that Ratzinger rules out the homily's application also to the original event – Adam is not an individual from the past, the "prison" is not the underworld, etc. Ratzinger simply does not acknowledge the real event of the descent. He jumps immediately to taking the homilist's moving portrayal as merely a metaphor for this life. However, the homily is not only a spiritual exhortation; it is also a catechesis. Indeed, its worth as an exhortation is undermined precisely to the extent that it is not based on a real event. For if it does not reflect the essence of a real event, it is an arbitrary story, and why should it be told that way rather than another?

Two collapses of descent and resurrection also appear later in the text. In one, Ratzinger points out that the early Church used those words, "I did not make you for the dungeon," in baptisms: "[The words express] the fact that Easter, the victory in which Jesus Christ breaks down the walls of alienation and leads us out into the open air, is to be heard continually in the sacrament of baptism."[49] Here Easter is the breaking of these walls, yet in Ratzinger's opening meditation on the icon, that was represented as occurring in the descent. Might different "walls" be broken by descent and resurrection, or might both descent and resurrection contribute to the breaking of the same "wall"? Either way, descent and resurrection ought not be collapsed, because they would be distinguished by their respective "walls" or by their respective contribution.

The other collapse is at the end of his meditation. Ratzinger writes,

> Christ summons us to find heaven in him, to discover him in others and thus to be heaven to each other. . . . Jesus stretches out his hand to us in his Easter message, in the mystery of the sacraments, so that Easter may be *now*, so that the light of heaven may shine forth in this world and the doors be opened.[50]

In each collapse, something the icon, homily, and indeed traditional Christian theology relate to the descent (the images of the breaking of the walls and the stretching out of the hand, the conferral of heaven) is im-

49. Ratzinger, "Christ the Liberator," 126.
50. Ratzinger, "Christ the Liberator," 128, emphasis in original.

mediately ascribed to Easter and interpreted in its significance for us the living; the descent and its own meaning for the dead and for the living is left unaddressed.

The reference to baptism makes oversight of the descent all the more puzzling, given the well-developed theological connections between the two, especially in the early Church. To be sure, one "rises to new life" from the baptismal font, but only if one has previously "descended" into it. St. Paul hints at the unique significance of that descent in his theology of being "*buried* [with Christ] by baptism" (Rom 6:4) and consequently "*dead* to sin" (Rom 6:11). Of course, to be fair to Ratzinger, no writer can discuss everything related to a topic. Just as the baptism-descent connection cannot be fully explored here,[51] neither could it be in his short meditation. Still, it is striking in a piece like his, which opens with two rich theological sources on the descent, that the descent itself is so completely sidestepped.

In all three meditations from *Behold the Pierced One*, Ratzinger emphasizes that the descent is a dimension of Christ's Easter victory. However, in them he also uses reference to the descent to stand either for Christ's embrace of His passion (first meditation) or for His resurrection (second and third), which are the topics he actually goes on to discuss. (In effect, he uses the literary technique called *metonymy*.) As a result, these reflections leave the reader wondering about Christ's historical descent and its own significance.

* * *

The fact that such perplexity is a rather consistent consequence of the texts examined in this chapter no doubt reflects Ratzinger's admitted hesitation to commit himself on what happened in Christ's descent, preferring to leave it in "mysterious obscurity." Whatever the cause, from an historical standpoint, Ratzinger's earliest assertions about the descent emphasized that Christ brings His own communion into death (as event or resultant state). After an interlude of interpreting the "descent" as a psychological experience prior to death, Ratzinger both increasingly saw the descent associated with Christ's resurrection and reaffirmed his initial approach. Language motifs similar to Balthasar's appear in far more circumspect contexts in Ratzinger and are supplemented by distinctly non-Balthasarian characteristics, which

51. A fuller introduction to the baptism–descent connection may be found in Pitstick, *Light in Darkness*, 40-46.

are essential for their interpretation. All these features militate against incautious assumptions of agreement between the two, especially given Ratzinger's admission that he could not in 1997, or ever before, wholly concur with Balthasar.

Edward T. Oakes has claimed that Balthasar's "most important ally" is Ratzinger.[52] Doubtful help is to be had from this alliance when Ratzinger himself said he could not fully agree with Balthasar, an admission Oakes omits. Moreover, in his treatment of Ratzinger's *Introduction to Christianity*, Oakes omits the important context Ratzinger provided by his use of Psalm 22 and Käsemann, his careful qualification of God's absence as "seeming," and his reflection on loneliness. Oakes simply relies upon the similarity of *some* of Balthasar's and Ratzinger's language, without attending to their important conceptual differences. Meanwhile, he completely ignores John Paul II's theology, which we will examine here in chapter 4.

Although Ratzinger said he did not know everything or even much about the meaning of Christ's descent, one thing he did know was that he did *not* agree fully with Balthasar. The available texts actually do not show any agreement in substance. Certainly neither of Ratzinger's proposals (Christ's pre-death psychological anguish of soul, and Christ's transformation of human death through bringing His own communion into it) reproduces Balthasar's post-death God-abandonment of the "naked" Person of the Son.

***Table 1.** Ratzinger on Christ's Descent before His Election as Benedict XVI*

"Meditations on Holy Week" (1967)—Overview from 1997 Introduction to "Meditations"	The creedal article may simply mean Christ died. The state after death is ultimate solitude. Christ brings His own communion into it. The Incarnation remains intact.
—First Meditation	"Death of God" theology and reductionism in faith life are placed in an analogy with the silence and emptiness of the disciples after Christ's burial. He does not discuss Christ's descent, but focuses instead on Christians' sense of God's absence.
—Second Meditation	Death (as dying? as resultant state?) is loneliness. Christ overcomes it by entering it as love.

52. Edward T. Oakes, S.J., "*Descensus* and Development: A Response to Recent Rejoinders," *International Journal of Systematic Theology*, 13, no. 1 (January, 2011): 12.

—Third Meditation	Christ enters into safety after His death. Holy Saturday shares in Easter and eschatological glory.
Introduction to Christianity (1968)	God's revelatory silence and Christ's use of the opening words of Ps 22 from the cross are departure points. Christ's abandonment by God is only apparent. Christ's "descent" occurs before death. The "descent" is Christ's sharing the human experience of radical loneliness at death. Christ's entrance as love into that loneliness overthrows it. Christ suffers in His humanity (and so, implicitly, the Incarnation remains intact).
Eschatology (1977)	Metaphorical vocabulary echoes some of Balthasar's, but it is ambiguous or context gives it a different meaning. Christ suffers in His humanity (and so, implicitly, the Incarnation remains intact).
"The Passover of Jesus and the Church" (1981, updated and published 1984)	The descent is entrance into death and the grave; what lies beyond is transformed by Christ's presence. As freely accepted by Christ, Christ's passion and descent are already victory.
"Taking Bearings in Christology" (1982, updated and published 1984)	Christ's last words change the event of death from destruction of communication into self-communication.
"The Lamb Redeemed the Sheep" (1984)	The descent is death and Christ is the true Lazarus, who returns from death in His resurrection. The descent is important due to its significance for the resurrection: it means Jesus rose *from death.*
"Christ the Liberator" (1984)	That Christ descended is significant because it means He rose. Mention of the descent is the occasion for discussing the victory of the resurrection.
Introduction to "Meditations" (1997)	He never fully agreed with Balthasar on Christ's descent. He prefers to leave the creedal article obscure. He reaffirms the general approach of the 1967 Meditations (see "Overview" above).

Spirit of the Liturgy (2000)	Descent and resurrection are linked as events of the new life wrought in Christ.
God Is Near Us (2001)	In "the abyss of death," Christ was not separated from the presence of God.

Table 2. Differences between Balthasar and Ratzinger on Christ's Descent

Balthasar	**Ratzinger**
Christ's descent occurs *after death.*	As treated in different texts, Christ's "descent" occurs *before death* or *is the event of death itself,* or the descent occurs *after death.*
Christ's abandonment by God is *real.*	Christ's abandonment by God is only *apparent.*
Christ descends in virtue of His *divinity.*	Christ descends in virtue of His *humanity.*
Christ descends to *intratrinitarian God-abandonment ("Sheol," in Balthasar's sense).*	Christ "descends" into *psychological anxiety, a "night" of the soul, or what would be loneliness for us.*
Christ suffers *union with, and punishment for, all sin.*	Christ suffers the *human psychological anguish at the approach of death.*
Christ *undergoes alienation* in the abode of the dead.	Christ *brings His own communion* into the abode of the dead.
The Incarnation is *suspended* in the descent.	The Incarnation remains *intact* in the descent and after death.

3

RATZINGER ON THE DESCENT AFTER HIS ELECTION AS BENEDICT XVI

We turn now to look at Ratzinger's engagement with Christ's descent after his election as Pope Benedict XVI. While Benedict's comments bear marks of continuity with his past in his attention to Christ's human soul and Christ's transformative entrance into the realm of the dead, we will see that his papal discussions also differ from his earlier work in important respects. Overall, they move even further away from Balthasar than Ratzinger had before his election.

Spe salvi (2007)

Perhaps best known are Benedict XVI's comments in his encyclical, *Spe salvi* (*Saved in Hope*), #37: in the context of urging us to seek healing not by fleeing suffering, but rather by accepting it with love through union with Christ, Benedict quotes at some length a letter from a 19th-century martyr in a concentration camp. Among other things, Paul Le-Bao-Tinh writes, "In the midst of these torments, which usually terrify others, I am, by the grace of God, full of joy and gladness, because I am not alone — Christ is with me."[1] The pope describes the letter as one from "'hell,'" in scare quotes, but one that also reveals the truth of the words of Psalm 138(139), "If I sink to the nether world, you are present there . . . for you darkness itself is not dark, and night shines as day." He ends the paragraph by saying, "Christ descended

1. Quoted in Benedict XVI, *Spe salvi* (November 30, 2007), #37.

into 'hell'" — again *hell* is in scare quotes — "and is therefore close to those cast into it, transforming their darkness into light."[2] The careful enclosure of *hell* in quotation marks indicates in both cases it is not to be understood as hell properly speaking.

Spe salvi #37 is an assertion of Christ's nearness to us in our sufferings in this life, which we metaphorically call hell. "My life is hell," we say. Really? While life in a concentration camp is more hellish than anything most of us probably go through, even it is still not the hell Christ characterized with eternal fire and the worm that never dies (e.g., Mt 25:41, Mk 9:48). Theologically, extending or applying a mystery of Christ's life to that of the faithful must be based directly on what happened to Christ Himself; in technical terms, the moral (or tropological) sense must be founded on the literal. Historically, the points that Christ understands our sufferings and is present to us in our darkest hours would have been made with reference to His crucifixion and the agonies that preceded it. In *Spe salvi*, Benedict does not say what happened in the descent professed in the creed. By omitting that and enclosing *hell* in scare quotes in the context of Le-Bao-Tinh's suffering *before death*, he only allows Christ's descent to "hell" to be taken in a metaphorical sense, namely, that Christ too suffered during His life such that He might have said, "That was hell." This approach fosters confusion, given that Christians also profess a real, historical descent. That the metaphor and the reality are distinct may be observed in the Italian: Benedict uses the singular *inferno*, but the creed uses the plural *inferi*. In addition, also speaking in Italian, his predecessor John Paul II had earlier made explicit that, in the creed, "The word 'hell' [*inferi*] does not mean the hell [*l'inferno*] of eternal damnation."[3]

Benedict makes his same point about God's closeness to us in our suffering — again in regard to the descent instead of the crucifixion, and again a metaphorical "descent into hell" instead of the historical one — in an address he gave when visiting Auschwitz in 2006. Referring to the Carmelite nuns who live their life of prayer nearby, he said that they know

> they are united in a special way to the mystery of Christ's Cross and [remind] us of the faith of Christians, which declares that God himself descended into the hell of suffering and suffers with us.[4]

2. Benedict XVI, *Spe salvi*, #37.

3. John Paul II, General Audience (January 11, 1989), #2.

4. Benedict XVI, Address on the Occasion of his Visit to the Auschwitz Camp (May 28, 2006).

Here the "mystery of Christ's Cross" seems identified with God's "descen[t] into the hell of suffering." This hell is not any abode of the afterlife, but rather the "hell" that suffering in this earthly life is, for He "suffers with us."[5] Benedict briefly mentions similar "descents" into suffering also in *Spe salvi*, #6; ***Verbum Domini*** (September 30, 2010), ##61, 106; and his **homily of June 11, 2010**. Although such conflation of cross, descent, and Christian suffering suggests these mysteries are all connected, as indeed they are, it does only that: suggests some connection, without shedding light on what the connection exactly is. What it could be depends in great measure upon what the historical descent was.

Easter Vigil Homily (2007)

What might that real event have been according to Benedict? In his homily for Easter Vigil, 2007, he at first appears to be more concrete. He opens again with Psalm 138(139), including the passages, "If I make my bed in Sheol, you are there! ... [Y]our right hand shall hold me . . . even the darkness is not dark to you." He applies the psalm as words Christ speaks first to the Father, unfolding them as, "Yes, I have journeyed to the uttermost depths of the earth, to the abyss of death, and brought them light; now I have risen and I am upheld for ever by your hands."[6] They are also words Christ speaks to us:

> My hand upholds you. Wherever you may fall, you will always fall into my hands. I am present even at the door of death. Where no one can accompany you further, and where you can bring nothing, even there I am waiting for you, and for you I will change darkness into light.[7]

When Benedict turns from the psalm to a closer treatment of the descent itself, he begins with his typical caution that on this side of death, we have no

5. Compare Ratzinger's "the hell of the concentration camps" and the other horrors that mark "the Good Friday of the twentieth century" in *Dogma and Preaching*, 33-35. Benedict's choice in quoting Le-Bao-Tinh's affirmation of Christ's nearness during his sufferings in the concentration camp also parallels other points he made more explicitly as Ratzinger in the same meditation in *Dogma and Preaching* (see p. 8 n. 4), a fact that is powerfully suggestive about what Benedict is doing in this part of *Spe salvi*.

6. Benedict XVI, Easter Vigil Homily (April 7, 2007).

7. Benedict XVI, Easter Vigil Homily, 2007.

knowledge of that other world. So, he says, "We can only imagine [Christ's] triumph over death with the help of images which remain very inadequate."[8] Benedict does not go on, however, to draw on the mystical dark night of the soul or on anything with overt echoes of Balthasar's soteriology. Instead, he first turns to the triumphal entrance hymn that is Psalm 23(24), a scriptural text extensively used in the early Church in connection with Christ's descent. He interprets its refrain of "Lift up your heads, O gates; be lifted up, O ancient doors!" as the gates of death being opened by Christ. Of the *Anastasis* icons, he then says, "The Easter icons of the Oriental Church *show* how Christ enters the world of the dead. He is clothed with light, for God is light."[9] Benedict next moves to the line from the Easter Vigil's Exultet, the poetic sequence proclaimed before the gospel reading, that recalls God's presence with the Israelites at night as a column of fire, "The night is bright as the day, the darkness is as light (cf. Ps 138[139]:12)." Continuing with words that recall the universal presentations of Christ's triumphal descent in earlier Church history, he says that Jesus enters the world of the dead bearing His stigmata as signs of the love that conquers death. There He clasps the hand of Adam and of the others waiting in death.

This approach is very different from Ratzinger's earlier work, and even more so from Balthasar's. Gone is Ratzinger's focus on silence, loneliness, and apparent abandonment. Continuity is seen, however, in that Christ brings God's light *with Him* into the abode of the dead. Benedict goes on to ask, "What is the meaning of all this imagery?" He answers by saying it shows that

> Only the Risen Christ can bring us to complete union with God. . . . Clinging to his Body we have life, and in communion with his Body we reach the very heart of God. Only thus is death conquered. . . . Love made Christ descend, and love is also the power by which he ascends. The power by which he brings us with him [sic]. In union with his love . . . let us descend with him into the world's darkness, knowing that in this way we will also rise up with him.[10]

8. Benedict XVI, Easter Vigil Homily, 2007.

9. Benedict XVI, Easter Vigil Homily, 2007, emphasis added. On the prevalence of Ps 23(24) in early Christian exegesis and the internal evidence that favors its interpretation as God's descent to the underworld, see Alan Cooper, "Ps 24:7-10: Mythology and Exegesis," *Journal of Biblical Literature* 102, no. 1 (1983): 37-60.

10. Benedict XVI, Easter Vigil Homily, 2007.

In this homily, the significance for Christian life is based more closely on an assertion of the literal meaning of Christ's descent, that is, on an assertion of what actually happened.

Still, as earlier, Benedict's commitment to what that event was remains unclear, because he calls his treatment of the descent "imagery": "We can only *imagine* his triumph over death with the help of *images* which remain very inadequate. . . . What is the meaning of all this *imagery*?"[11] Unless he meant that we take those images also as reality, Benedict never says what meaning the event had in the life of Christ Himself, what actually happened; his explanation of significance again is limited to the moral or tropological, that *we* would know Christ is our salvation.[12] His strongest suggestion of what the real event was, comes close to his reference to Psalm 138(139): "In the impenetrable gloom of death Christ came like light — the night became as bright as day and the darkness became as light."[13] If so, in what sense are the images inadequate? Are they inadequate as all our praise is inadequate to God's glory? Or are they inadequate, as Balthasar might say, because the Easter icons represent the absolute darkness and torment of Christ's God-abandonment with light because it was an event of divine love? Although such a Balthasarian reading cannot be derived from the text alone but would have to be supplied by a reader along the lines I have suggested, Benedict's treatment of the descent in terms of "images" makes it difficult to know clearly what he means to assert.

The salvific extent of Christ's descent is also left ambiguous. In one place, Benedict says Christ "meets Adam and all the men and women waiting in the night of death."[14] If Christ is both the only possible perfect fulfillment of human desire and mankind's ultimate judge, then in one sense all humanity, doomed to die, waits for Christ, including those who have rejected Him. In contrast, in the traditional understanding of the descent, the dead awaiting Christ were specifically only those who also during their lives had awaited with love His coming; that is, they had died in the grace of the faith, hope, and charity they possessed during life. Does Benedict mean this? Perhaps; he does say the "journey of the incarnation" is completed in Christ's descent into the common human fate of death, by which "he now clasps the hand of Adam, of every man and woman *who awaits him*, and brings them to the

11. Benedict XVI, Easter Vigil Homily, 2007, emphasis added.

12. Compare Ratzinger, "The Ascension of Christ," *Dogma and Preaching*, 60-65.

13. Benedict XVI, Easter Vigil Homily, 2007.

14. Benedict XVI, Easter Vigil Homily, 2007.

light."[15] Or does Benedict mean all, sheep and goats, meet Christ alike after death? Do they meet Him as judge? Or do they also meet Him, as Balthasar has it, as a presence that even in the hell of damnation can turn their hearts to accept God?[16] Although Benedict's homily certainly can and should be read as consistent with the Church's historical doctrine, the words themselves could be utilized to support the universalist hope for which Balthasar was known. This wider reading is perhaps supported by the fact that Benedict does not reference Eve by name as a person among those Christ meets while "Adam" is used as standing for the whole of humanity, a usage explicit when Benedict says, "In the incarnation, the Son of God became one with human beings — with Adam."[17]

The final feature to highlight about this homily is that in it Benedict also discusses baptism, which has been connected with Christ's descent and the Easter Vigil since apostolic times. Here again we find his emphasis on Christ bringing communion into death, and in this case, specifically to those united to Him:

> If we offer ourselves in this way, if we accept, as it were, the death of our very selves, this means that the frontier between death and life is no longer absolute. On either side of death we are with Christ and so, from that moment forward, death is no longer a real boundary. . . . In Baptism, in the company of Christ, we have already made that cosmic journey to the very abyss of death. At his side and, indeed, drawn up in his love, we are freed from fear. He enfolds us and carries us wherever we may go — he who is Life itself.[18]

Jesus of Nazareth, Volume 1 (2007)

In volume 1 of *Jesus of Nazareth*, the descent is again connected to baptism — this time Christ's own in the river Jordan, as has been the continual tradition of the Christian East. Although this work was published after Ratzinger was elected pope, according to Catholic custom its author is properly identified

15. Benedict XVI, Easter Vigil Homily, 2007, emphasis added.

16. See the exposition in Alyssa Lyra Pitstick, *Light in Darkness: Hans Urs von Balthasar and the Catholic Doctrine of Christ's Descent into Hell* (Grand Rapids: Eerdmans, 2007), 263-70.

17. Benedict XVI, Easter Vigil Homily, 2007.

18. Benedict XVI, Easter Vigil Homily, 2007.

as Ratzinger, and not as Benedict, because he wrote the book not as a papal act, but as a private theologian. He himself made that emphatically clear:

> It goes without saying that this book is in no way an exercise of the magisterium [ecclesial teaching authority], but is solely an expression of my personal search 'for the face of the Lord' (cf. Ps 27:8). Everyone is free, then, to contradict me.[19]

Now although Benedict in his Easter Vigil homily and Ratzinger in *Jesus of Nazareth* thus follows Sacred Tradition in linking baptism and descent, he diverges in the latter text by relating the parable of the overthrow of the strong man (Lk 11:22) only to Jesus's baptism and not at all to His descent.[20]

Moreover, his comments on the descent are again ambiguous. For example, in the treatment by Edward T. Oakes mentioned in the introduction, Oakes quotes a central early passage, here with my emphasis:

> Jesus' *Baptism*, then, is understood as a repetition of the whole of history, which both recapitulates the past and anticipates the future. His entering into the sin of others is a descent into the "inferno." But he does not descend merely in the role of a spectator, as in Dante's Inferno. Rather, he goes down in the role of one whose suffering-with-others is a transforming suffering that turns the underworld around, knocking down and flinging open the gates of the abyss. *His Baptism* is a descent into the house of the evil one. . . . [He] can take upon himself all the sin of the world and then suffer it through to the end — omitting nothing on the downward path into identity with the fallen.[21]

Here, as in *Spe salvi*, note the scare quotes around *inferno*. Contrary to how Oakes hopes to utilize this passage, it is not about the descent after Christ's death. The descent here is Christ's descent into the waters of the Jordan at His baptism and, *through that baptism*, "His entering into the sin of others" — whatever that means exactly. The character of this solidarity remains unclear,

19. Joseph Ratzinger, *From the Baptism in the Jordan to the Transfiguration*, vol. 1, *Jesus of Nazareth*, trans. Adrian J. Walker (New York: Doubleday, 2007), xxiii-xxiv. The English translation was published simultaneously with the German original in 2007.

20. Ratzinger, *From the Baptism*, 18-27.

21. Ratzinger, *From the Baptism*, 20, quoted in Edward T. Oakes, S.J., "*Descensus* and Development: A Response to Recent Rejoinders," *International Journal of Systematic Theology*, 13, no. 1 (January, 2011): 13-14, my emphasis and ellipsis.

for if Christ omits "nothing on the downward path into identity with the fallen," it is hardly credible that Ratzinger means *nothing* in a strict sense, for that would include the personal act of sin itself. Just what he means, he does not elaborate.

Read in context, Christ's descent after death appears in volume 1 of *Jesus of Nazareth* only in a remote way: First, Ratzinger connects (A) Jesus's baptism and (B) His descent: in describing Christ's baptism as an anticipation of His cross and resurrection, Ratzinger sees it implicitly anticipating also the descent that links that pair.[22] He goes on to connect (A) baptism, including the forgiveness of sins it foreshadows, to (C) the human experience of temptation: Christ's acceptance of solidarity with Adam's fallen race manifested through His baptism includes acceptance of the dangers of the human condition.[23] Finally, Ratzinger connects (B) Christ's descent with (C) His experience of our temptations. Importantly in this third step, Ratzinger does *not* mean that the suffering of temptation occurs in the descent after death but rather that temptation itself is a "'descen[t] into hell,' as it were."[24] The three themes of baptism, descent, and temptation are united by Ratzinger's explanation that, in biblical imagery, descent into a river (like the Jordan at Christ's baptism) represents a descent into death, because it is a descent into danger, as temptation also is.[25]

Yet again we must ask, What actually happened in Christ's own descent? One would anticipate that such a key to the full significance of volume 1's allusions to a "descent" would be provided in Ratzinger's more explicit treatment of the Passion in volume 2.

"Veneration of the Holy Shroud Meditation" (2010)

Since we have been following Ratzinger chronologically for the most part, let us turn from *Jesus of Nazareth* for a moment to consider Benedict XVI's meditation upon his veneration of the Shroud of Turin, May 2, 2010; it too leads us to a keen anticipation for that second volume. Benedict was prompted to reflect upon Christ's descent by the subtitle for the exposition of the Shroud, "The Mystery of Holy Saturday." His meditation is structured

22. Ratzinger, *From the Baptism*, 14-23.
23. Ratzinger, *From the Baptism*, 26-39, see also 160.
24. Ratzinger, *From the Baptism*, 161, see also 196.
25. On the river as danger and descent, see Ratzinger, *From the Baptism*, 239.

by three famous physical characteristics of the Shroud: the image of the crucified body, its photographic quality, and the blood stains upon it.

The Shroud, Benedict says, is "the Icon of Holy Saturday."[26] His naming it an icon is suggestive of how its visible physicality points beyond itself to realities of great significance invisible to the viewers of the icon. The first of these realities is not to be overlooked for its obviousness, namely, how Christ's body lay in the tomb after His death and before His resurrection. Benedict calls attention to this fact, but does not linger over it. It is, however, worth our pausing to observe that this testimony of the body's duration points to the reality of the Incarnation and, contra Balthasar, its permanence: the Son took upon Himself a real human nature and never repudiated it. Hence, even in the separation of body and soul that is death, the body, wrapped in the shroud in the tomb, continued to exist united to the Word, as did Christ's soul, a belief reaffirmed in the *Catechism of the Catholic Church* (#626). We saw in the previous chapter that Ratzinger had also earlier appeared attentive to the permanence of the Incarnation.

Benedict uses the ancient homily that is part of the Divine Office for Holy Saturday as his transition from the Shroud as evidence of Christ's entombed body to the heart of his reflection:

> Holy Saturday is the day when God remains hidden, we read in an ancient Homily: "What has happened? Today the earth is shrouded in deep silence, deep silence and stillness, profound silence because the King sleeps. . . . God has died in the flesh, and has gone down to rouse the realm of the dead" (*Homily on Holy Saturday, PG* 43, 439).[27]

Besides forming part of the Divine Office, this same homily is quoted at length also in the sections on Christ's descent in John Paul II's audience of April 3, 1996, and in the *Catechism of the Catholic Church* (#635); it is, in other words, something of a touchstone for recent magisterial treatments of the descent. We saw Ratzinger using it also before his election in his third meditation in *Behold the Pierced One*. The selected passage and ellipsis here are Benedict's own, and his choice of what he quoted is highly significant for his meditation.

Its major theme is one that has interested him since his teaching days: God's hidden presence in silence. In *Introduction to Christianity* Ratzinger

26. Benedict XVI, "Veneration of the Holy Shroud Meditation" (May 2, 2010).
27. Benedict XVI, "Veneration of the Holy Shroud Meditation."

highlighted our twofold experience of God's silence as both the apparent absence of word and the place of revelation, going on to emphasize Christ's closeness to us (revelation) in the most challenging loneliness (absence), that of approaching death. Without abandoning that perspective, Benedict's meditation shows a subtle shift: here the two facets of God's hiddenness in silence are His death in the flesh, which the living must confront, and His transformation of the realm of the dead.

These two, God's seeming absence to the living and His revelatory presence to the dead, are paralleled in the way the Shroud of Turin acts as both a photographic negative and a positive image. The "photographic negative" side of God's hiddenness is contemporary spirituality's sense, in the face of the horrors of the last century, of a great interior void. In this context, Benedict recalls Nietzsche's famous cry, which seems to summarize this sensibility, "God is dead! And we killed him!" This facet echoes Ratzinger's thoughts in the first of his "Meditations on Holy Week": in the meditation before the Shroud, once again the dreariness and "negative" side is what the *living* experience, similar to what the apostles felt on the first Holy Saturday.

Yet there is a "positive" side to the death of the incarnate Son of God, and it has to do with what happened to *Christ* and what He did on Holy Saturday:

> In this "time-beyond-time," Jesus Christ "descended to the dead." [The Italian here, *inferi*, would have been rendered *hell* in earlier translations.] What do these words mean? They mean that God, having made himself man, reached the point of entering man's most extreme and absolute solitude, where not a ray of love enters, where total abandonment reigns without any word of comfort: "hell" [*inferi*].[28]

As we have seen before in Ratzinger's work, Benedict here begins with language that sounds very much like Balthasar. Indeed, this mediation may be his most Balthasarian-sounding text on the descent. Perhaps that is even appropriate: as a meditation, Benedict may have given himself freer rein to express his personal spirituality than in more authoritative texts. However that may be, we will again see that he takes it in a different direction from Balthasar. He does that partly by again stressing that this descent is a function of Christ's humanity ("having made himself man") and partly by again enclosing *hell* in scare quotes. Benedict continues,

28. Benedict XVI, "Veneration of the Holy Shroud Meditation."

> Jesus Christ, by remaining in death, passed beyond the door of this ultimate solitude to lead us too to cross it with him. We have all, at some point, felt the frightening sensation of abandonment, and that is what we fear most about death, just as when we were children we were afraid to be alone in the dark and could only be reassured by the presence of a person who loved us. Well, this is exactly what happened on Holy Saturday: the voice of God resounded in the realm of death. The unimaginable occurred: namely, Love penetrated "hell". Even in the extreme darkness of the most absolute human loneliness we may hear a voice that calls us and find a hand that takes ours and leads us out. Human beings live because they are loved and can love; and if love even penetrated the realm of death, then life also even reached there. In the hour of supreme solitude we shall never be alone: *Passio Christi. Passio hominis.* [The Passion of Christ. The passion of man.][29]

Since parallelism in this second use of "hell" demands that it be understood as "the realm of death," that may also be the sense intended in the first section of the quotation just above. Such usage would echo the broadness of the creed's "*ad inferos*" (He descended to "those below"). Alone, both the creed's term and Benedict's second usage are too indefinite to specify which abode of the dead is intended; neither immediately signify the hell of eternal punishment. In that case, the state of death in general, and not as specific punishment for personal sin, seems intended. Although Benedict describes hell more chillingly in the first section, to understand that abandonment to characterize the end point of Christ's descent would set Benedict in contradiction with the *Roman Catechism* (also known as the *Catechism of the Council of Trent*), which is explicit that Christ descended to souls who "without experiencing any sort of pain, but supported by the blessed hope of redemption . . . enjoyed peaceful repose,"[30] and with John Paul II, who, as mentioned earlier, clarified that in the creed, "the word 'hell' does not mean the hell of eternal damnation."[31]

Another possible interpretation, one that does not entail those conflicts, is that the love and comfort cut off is that of the communion among living humanity. This reading is more consistent with Ratzinger's tendency

29. Benedict XVI, "Veneration of the Holy Shroud Meditation."

30. *Catechism of the Council of Trent*, trans. John A. McHugh, O.P., and Charles J. Callan, O.P. (Rockford, IL: Tan, 1982), 63.

31. John Paul II, General Audience (January 11, 1989), #2.

to emphasize that dimension for the dying person and to project it also into the afterlife. Benedict is, after all, talking about how "what *we* fear most about death" is abandonment, or loneliness, which recalls to the reader's mind Ratzinger's early exposition in his *Introduction to Christianity*. The same elements appear there: death as loss of communion and the overthrow of what would be loneliness for us through Love's transformative presence.

In the case of Benedict's meditation on the Shroud, that transformation is expressed this way:

> This is the mystery of Holy Saturday! Truly from there, from the darkness of the death of the Son of God, the light of a new hope gleamed: the light of the Resurrection. . . . [Those who see the Shroud] indeed see the death of Jesus, but they also see his Resurrection; in the bosom of death, life is now vibrant, since love dwells within it.[32]

So, though Christ enters death, "man's most extreme and absolute solitude . . . where total abandonment reigns without any word of comfort," He does so bringing comfort with Him. He transforms the realm He enters.

Benedict closes his meditation focusing on life and connecting it through the bloodstains on the Shroud to his theme of God's hiddenness in silence. He says,

> [The Shroud] speaks with blood, and blood is life! The Shroud is an Icon written in blood; the blood of a man . . . whose right side was pierced. . . . That blood and that water speak of life. It is like a spring that murmurs in the silence, and . . . we can listen to it in the silence of Holy Saturday.[33]

The emphasis here on the life and light of the Resurrection shining in the very realm of death is another departure from Balthasar, one seen even before Ratzinger's election in his third "Meditation on Holy Week" about Holy Saturday. In that context, we heard some of the pointed words Balthasar had for the icons of the Christian East that manifest the resurrection in this way; one wonders how he regarded Holy Saturday's Divine Office, which catalyzed this reflection of Benedict on the Shroud?

32. Benedict XVI, "Veneration of the Holy Shroud Meditation."
33. Benedict XVI, "Veneration of the Holy Shroud Meditation."

Benedict's meditation on the Shroud, including his significant choice of quoted material from the Holy Saturday Liturgy of the Hours, is consistent with Ratzinger/Benedict's earlier indications that Christ's sufferings occurred before His death and "in the flesh," that is, in His human nature. In this way and also by suggesting that the descent following the moment of death entails an exercise of life-giving power, Benedict's view contrasts with Balthasar's insistence that Christ's passion continues in His descent until He experiences in His own divine Person the spiritual death that is abandonment by the Father. There is no evidence in Benedict that his frequent references to the light Christ manifests in His descent are to be understood as this agony of God-forsakenness that Balthasar thinks is redemptive and so life-giving. Indeed, there is evidence to the contrary when we recall how Benedict *contrasts* the darkness of death with Christ's dwelling in it on Holy Saturday as the light, life, and communion of the Resurrection.

As in *Spe salvi* and his 2007 Easter homily, however, Benedict's language here is metaphorical and he speaks in images: there is the door, the voice, the hand, the penetration of "hell" by Love, etc. Again he does not say concretely what happened to Christ in His descent. Even when he says, "This is exactly what happened on Holy Saturday," he does not say exactly, but continues with a metaphor: "The voice of God resounded in the realm of death"! It is also difficult to understand what he is asserting about Christ's descent as such, as opposed to what came before it, because his treatment blurs the experience of dying, the moment of death, and what comes after. Given Ratzinger's earlier hesitations to speculate about anything beyond the event of death, this meditation before the Shroud marks a new step in that Benedict claims to attend to what happened to Christ in the descent. Other than his contrast of Christ's presence as light with the darkness of the realm of death, however, he actually instead consistently emphasizes the significance of the descent for the living: as in Ratzinger's *Introduction to Christianity*, we are reassured of Christ's presence in the moments of our greatest fears, particularly that of death.

Jesus of Nazareth, Volume 2 (2011)

Having read the Shroud meditation and the allusions Ratzinger made to the descent in volume 1 of *Jesus of Nazareth,* one might have hoped that greater clarity would be provided in volume 2, which treats Jesus's entrance into Jerusalem through His resurrection. In that second volume, however, Ratzinger does not discuss the descent at all!

The cry of abandonment is again understood as Christ's prayer of Psalm 22, but without mention of descent, the loneliness of death, or anguish at its approach, as found in his earlier interpretations. Instead, Ratzinger takes as interpretative key the patristic reading of the psalms as prayers of "corporate personality," that is, as Christ praying both as head and body, thus uniting *our* suffering to Himself.[34] Rather than Balthasar's extension of *Christ's sufferings* after His death, Ratzinger highlights how expanding the number of the *persons* in whom the psalm is said increases the scope of the "horror of [Christ's] Passion."[35] Despite that increased scope, Ratzinger again emphasizes the unique communion Christ establishes: "Yet at the same time, Jesus' suffering is a Messianic Passion. It is suffering in fellowship with us and for us, in a solidarity — born of love — that already includes redemption, the victory of love."[36]

Another important difference from his earliest approach in *Introduction to Christianity* is that Ratzinger discusses Christ's fear and anguish in connection to Gethsemane, rather than to the cross. Part of Christ's distress is "the primordial fear of created nature in the face of imminent death, and yet there is more" — and here we find language reminiscent of Balthasar:

> [It is] the particular horror felt by him who is Life itself before the abyss of the full power of destruction, evil, and enmity with God that is now unleashed upon him, and he now takes directly upon himself, or rather into himself, to the point that he is "made to be sin" (cf. 2 Cor 5:21).
>
> Because he is the Son, he sees with total clarity the whole foul flood of evil. . . . Because he is the Son, he experiences deeply all the horror, filth, and baseness that he must drink from the "chalice" prepared for him: the vast power of sin and death. All this he must take into himself, so that it can be disarmed and defeated in him.[37]

34. Joseph Ratzinger, *Holy Week: From the Entrance into Jerusalem to the Resurrection*, vol. 2, *Jesus of Nazareth*, trans. Philip J. Whitmore (San Francisco: Ignatius, 2011), 215. The English translation was published simultaneously with the German original in 2011.

35. Ratzinger, *Holy Week*, 216.

36. Ratzinger, *Holy Week*, 216.

37. Ratzinger, *Holy Week*, 155.

"Here the abyss of sin and evil penetrated deep with his soul."[38] "And he takes injustice upon himself; he shoulders the destructive burden of guilt."[39]

It is certainly true that only One who is God can know just what an outrage and tragedy death and sin are.[40] And certainly Christ expiated in His own innocent person the guilt of the world. But, as the Church Fathers would have asked, in virtue of which of His two natures? How are we to understand the taking of "enmity with God . . . into himself," into One who is God, so as to be "made to be sin"? This expression is very close to Balthasar's "literally 'made sin.'"

Ratzinger does not mean to go nearly so far. Drawing upon Albert Vanhoye's work on Hebrews 5, Ratzinger's answer lies in a profound meditation on the obedience of Christ in Gethsemane as His priestly sacrifice:

> In Jesus' natural human will, the sum total of human nature's resistance to God is, as it were, present within Jesus himself. The obstinacy of us all, the whole of our opposition to God is present, and in his struggle, Jesus elevates our recalcitrant nature to become its real self.[41]

For in Christ's offer and gift of Himself through obedience, the human will is drawn into the Son's filial deference to the Father. In His bearing our resistance to that point, "we are all drawn into sonship."[42]

Ratzinger has integrated Balthasar's *language*, but *not its content*, with the doctrine that because Christ had two natures, He had two wills, one divine, one human: thus, if the essence of sin is to say no to God out of fear of the implications of complete submission to Him, then Christ could experience the temptation to sin in His human will. The "abyss of enmity to God" is the resistance of fallen human nature, not something abstract and personified like Balthasar's "sin as such." If Christ prayed Psalm 22 on the cross as Head of the suffering body of humanity, He could likewise have struggled with the human temptation not to offer "the body [God] has prepared for us"[43] in obedience. This reading is confirmed in Ratzinger's reflection on Hebrews 10, where he highlights how Christ did indeed offer His body and thus how

38. Ratzinger, *Holy Week*, 149.

39. Ratzinger, *Holy Week*, 150.

40. On Christ's distress at death specifically, see Ratzinger, *Holy Week*, 163.

41. Ratzinger, *Holy Week*, 161. The reflection on Christ's consecration in His obedience is pp. 157-66.

42. Ratzinger, *Holy Week*, 161.

43. Par. Heb 10:6. See Ratzinger, *Holy Week*, 233-35.

in the Eucharist, "The Lord's obedience on the Cross . . . draws us into the perfect worship [He] offered."[44]

The deepest influence for Ratzinger's reflection here may not be Balthasar, but John Paul II. In the latter's general audience of October 19, 1988, a number of significantly similar things are said, especially this passage:

> St. Paul says of Christ that he "became obedient unto death, even death on a cross" (Phil 2:8). He thus reached the extreme limit of self-emptying included in the Incarnation of the Son of God, in contrast with the disobedience of Adam who had desired to "grasp" equality with God (cf. Phil 2:6). . . .
>
> At Gethsemane we see how painful this obedience was to be: "Father, all things are possible to you; remove this cup from me; yet not what I will, but what you will" (Mk 14:36). In that moment Christ's agony of soul was much more painful than that of the body (cf. Summa Theol., III, q. 46, a. 6). This was because of the interior conflict between the supreme motives of the passion in the divine plan, and the perception which Jesus, in the refined sensitivity of his soul, had of the abominable filth of sin. Sin seems to have been poured over him, who had become as it were "sin" (that is, the victim of sin) as St. Paul says (cf. 2 Cor 5:21), so that universal sin might be expiated in him. Thus Jesus arrived at death as at the supreme act of obedience: "Father, into your hands I commit my spirit" (Lk 23:46): the spirit, that is, the principle of his human life.
>
> Suffering and death are the definitive manifestation of the Son's total obedience to the Father. The incarnate Word's homage and sacrifice of obedience are a marvelous demonstration of filial availability, which in the mystery of the Incarnation rises up and in a certain way penetrates the mystery of the Trinity! With the perfect homage of his obedience Jesus Christ obtained a complete victory over the disobedience of Adam and over all the rebellions which can arise in human hearts, more especially because of suffering and death. Here also it can be said that "where sin increased, grace abounded all the more" (Rom 5:20). Jesus made up for the disobedience which is always included in human sin, by satisfying on our behalf the demands of divine justice.[45]

44. Ratzinger, *Holy Week*, 235.

45. John Paul II, General Audience (October 19, 1988), ##5-6. The paragraphs in the

Here John Paul II says Christ is "made sin," not in Balthasar's sense, but as being a "victim of sin," that is, in the sense of the definitive offering to expiate sins that fulfills and surpasses the sacrifices prescribed by the Law in the Old Testament. It is Christ's self-offering in obedience that heals the disobedience constitutive of all sin. It is by His perfect obedience as man, accepting even the death of the cross, that He satisfies all justice, rather than through what Balthasar describes as the Son's union with sin-in-itself and consequent suffering of the eternal punishment of something worse than hell. Indeed, in his very next audience, John Paul II explicitly states that justice as somehow satisfied because "an innocent person has suffered the chastisement merited by the guilty" is not justice at all, but rather "a grave injustice."[46]

If we assume that John Paul II has provided inspiration for Ratzinger with his October 19 audience, we see that Ratzinger has developed it by drawing out just how Christ's obedience might rectify sin and by clarifying the priestly character of Christ's self-offering. Ratzinger has also added another sense in which Christ is the "victim" of sin, in that He is assaulted by its possibility and all it means through the experience of temptation.

It is worth a digression to see confirmation of the shift after Ratzinger's election in his interpretation of Psalm 22, which is found in some more recent treatments of Christ's words from the cross by Benedict. First, in Benedict's audience of September 14, 2011, he is specific about what kind of suffering it was that the psalm expressed for Christ; he is also explicit that it manifested Christ's abiding confidence in God:

> [The initial cry of the psalm, recorded in Matthew and Mark] expresses all the desolation of the Messiah, Son of God, who is facing the drama of death, a reality totally opposed to the Lord of life. Forsaken by almost all his followers, betrayed and denied by the disciples, surrounded by people who insult him, Jesus is under the crushing weight of a mission that was to pass through humiliation and annihilation [*l'annichilimento*; perhaps *devastation* would have been a preferable translation, as Jesus was not literally annihilated]. This is why he cried out to the Father, and his suffering took up the sorrowful words of the Psalm. But his is not a desperate cry, nor was that of the Psalmist who, in his supplication,

English translation online are unnumbered; the paragraph numbers given refer to those in the Italian original.

46. John Paul II, General Audience (October 26, 1988), #4.

> takes a tormented path which nevertheless opens out at last into a perspective of praise, into trust in the divine victory.
>
> And since in the Jewish custom citing the beginning of a Psalm implied a reference to the whole poem, although Jesus' anguished prayer retains its burden of unspeakable suffering, it unfolds to the certainty of glory. "Was it not necessary that the Christ should suffer these things and enter into his glory?", the Risen Christ was to say to the disciples at Emmaus (Lk 24:26).[47]

Similarly, in reflecting on Jesus's last words in the Gospel of Luke during his audience February 15, 2012, Benedict comments on Christ's trust and confidence in God amid His sufferings before He died:

> At this moment of suffering Jesus' prayer, "Father into your hands I commit my spirit", is a loud cry of supreme and total entrustment to God. This prayer expresses the full awareness that he had not been abandoned.
>
> ... Jesus' prayer as he faces death is dramatic as it is for every human being but, at the same time, it is imbued with that deep calmness that is born from trust in the Father and from the desire to commend oneself totally to him.[48]

Note here as well that the suffering Jesus is undergoing is, as I have argued from the beginning with Ratzinger, the human anguish at the approach of death.

Finally, just a week prior to his reflection on Christ's last words in Luke, Benedict gave his most extended treatment of Psalm 22 on Christ's lips in his General Audience of February 8, 2012, as he considered it again in the context of the Gospels of Matthew and Mark. What is striking? First of all, with a repeated insistence that demands attention, everywhere throughout the audience Benedict refers to Jesus's cry as a prayer. In fact, it is never mentioned without somehow being called a prayer. The reason becomes evident as Benedict underscores — again, with frequent repetition — that the Father only seems to be absent, that the abandonment is only apparent. Even the darkness that covers the earth at the crucifixion is a sign of God's presence that recalls the theophanies of Exodus and Deuteron-

47. Benedict XVI, General Audience (Sept. 14, 2011).
48. Benedict XVI, General Audience (Feb. 15, 2012).

omy.[49] Though the Father's voice is not heard as at Jesus's baptism and transfiguration, though silence falls at the approach of the human death of the Incarnate Word, yet "the Father's loving gaze is fixed on his Son's gift of love."[50] Moreover, the Son knows it: "Jesus is utterly certain of the closeness of the Father who approves this supreme act of love."[51] Hence His cry is a prayer because it is spoken to Someone, to God, to the One who hears, to Him who is near.

As in the Gospel of Luke, Christ's cry in Matthew and Mark is not just a prayer, but specifically a prayer of trust in the midst of suffering. In contrast to His rejection and abandonment by men, His own "extreme trust and his abandonment into God's hands"[52] is expressed in His prayer. "Jesus gives vent to his heart's grief, but at the same time makes clear the meaning of the Father's presence and his consent to the Father's plan of salvation of humanity."[53]

What is the cause of this grief? Benedict refers to Jesus's suffering in this hour along the lines of Ratzinger's pre-death "descent": His anguish is not the beginning of Balthasar's God-abandonment and wrath, but "the human drama of death."[54] He suffers "in communion with us and for us"; He "took upon himself our sufferings, to carry them together with us and to give us the firm hope that they will be overcome (cf. Encyclical Letter *Spe salvi*, nn. 35-40)."[55] This parenthetical reference is highly significant for our study because it includes *Spe salvi*, #37, the paragraph in which Benedict used Le-Bao-Tinh's letter to speak of Christ's descent into "hell" (in scare quotes). In other words, Benedict here provides an interpretative key that confirms he is using the "descent" in *Spe salvi*, #37 as a metaphor for our sufferings rather than speaking of Christ's historical descent after His death.

Lastly, Christ's prayer of Psalm 22 is one on behalf of all humanity. Benedict again sees the psalm as prayed in what he earlier called "corporate personality," an interpretation taken also by the *Catechism of the Catholic Church* (#603), which he cites in this audience. As Benedict says,

49. Benedict XVI, General Audience (Feb. 8, 2012).
50. Benedict XVI, General Audience (Feb. 8, 2012).
51. Benedict XVI, General Audience (Feb. 8, 2012).
52. Benedict XVI, General Audience (Feb. 8, 2012).
53. Benedict XVI, General Audience (Feb. 8, 2012).
54. Benedict XVI, General Audience (Feb. 8, 2012).
55. Benedict XVI, General Audience (Feb. 8, 2012).

> Jesus makes his own the whole of Psalm 22 (21), the Psalm of the suffering people of Israel. *In this way* he takes upon himself not only the sin of his people, but also that of all men and women who are suffering from the oppression of evil and, at the same time, he places all this before God's own heart, in the certainty that his cry will be heard in the Resurrection.[56]

Here Benedict reiterates that "Jesus' prayer is not the cry of one who meets death with despair,"[57] for He makes the *whole* of the psalm His, and the psalm ends in confidence and joy. Hence He has "certainty that his cry will be heard." Here also Benedict clarifies how Christ "takes sin upon Himself" along the lines of the high priestly sacrifice he described in *Jesus of Nazareth*, vol. 2: not only by sharing in human suffering, but by doing so in trusting obedience, Jesus offers prayer and a sacrifice of praise (the twofold structure of Ps 22) on behalf of His people, all humanity.

The twin features of suffering and commitment are common to Benedict's treatment of Christ's prayer of Psalm 22 and Ratzinger's discussion of Gethsemane in volume 2 of *Jesus of Nazareth*, to our general examination of which we can now return. As we have said, Ratzinger does not treat Christ's descent in volume 2 of *Jesus of Nazareth*. However, his reflections on Gethsemane and what he says about the burial and resurrection are suggestive of the descent theology that would be compatible.

The anointing of Christ's body planned by the women is "an attempt to hold death at bay, to preserve the corpse from decomposition. And yet [theirs] is a vain attempt."[58] On Easter, however, "they will see that Jesus is not to be held captive by death. . . . God has preserved him from decomposition in a definite way."[59] This same emphasis on the definitive preservation from corruption appears in Ratzinger's treatment of the resurrection based on Peter's Pentecost sermon (Acts 2:26-28), especially its quotation of Psalm 16:8-10: ". . . my flesh will dwell in hope. For you will not abandon my soul

56. Benedict XVI, General Audience (Feb. 8, 2012), emphasis added. In these two audiences (September 14, 2011, and February 8, 2012), Benedict reaffirms observations he made as Ratzinger as early as 1973 in *Dogma and Preaching* about Christ's cry being a prayer and about His suffering on the cross uniting Him with all others who are afflicted; see p. 8 n. 4.

57. Benedict XVI, General Audience (Feb. 8, 2012).

58. Ratzinger, *Holy Week*, 229.

59. Ratzinger, *Holy Week*, 229.

to Hades, nor let your Holy One see corruption."[60] Finally, Ratzinger will significantly say that in the resurrection appearances, "Jesus comes *from the realm of pure life*, from God; he comes as the one who is truly alive, *who is himself the source of life*."[61] The repeated denials of any form of decay and these last assertions of definitive life imply that nothing of Christ — neither human body nor human soul, neither divine nature nor divine Person — underwent corruption in His descent. Ratzinger's position contrasts in a fundamental way with that of Balthasar, for whom the Son is denuded of both human and divine attributes to be united with the corruption of sin-in-itself.

"In His Image" Italian Television Interview (2011)

Benedict's last text to consider to date (April, 2012) is his response during an Italian television program, "In His Image: Questions about Jesus." The question was asked, "What is Jesus doing in the time between His death and resurrection? Seeing that [the creed says He descended into hell], should we think that that will also happen to us, after death, before going to heaven?" The pope responded,

> First of all, this descent of Jesus' soul should not be imagined as a geographical or a spatial trip, from one continent to another. It is the soul's journey. We have to remember that Jesus' soul always touches the Father, it is always in contact with the Father but, at the same time, this human soul extends to the very borders [*ultimi confini*] of the human being. *In this sense* it goes into the depths, into the lost places, to where all who do not arrive at their life's goal go, thus transcending the continents of the past. This word about the Lord's descent into Hell [*Inferi*] mainly means that Jesus reaches even the past, that the effectiveness of the Redemption does not begin in the year 0 or 30, but also goes to the past, embraces the past, all men and women of all time. The Church Fathers say, with a very beautiful image, that Jesus takes Adam and Eve, that is, humanity, by the hand and guides them forward, guides them on high. He thus creates access to God because humanity on its own cannot arrive at God's level. He himself, being man, can take humanity by the hand and open the access. To what? To the reality we call Heaven. So

60. Ratzinger, *Holy Week*, 255.
61. Ratzinger, *Holy Week*, 269, emphasis added.

> this descent into Hell [*Inferi*], that is, into the depth of the human being, into humanity's past, is an essential part of Jesus' mission, of His mission as Redeemer, and does not apply to us. Our lives are different. We are already redeemed by the Lord and we arrive before the Judge, after our death, under Jesus' gaze. On one hand, this gaze will be purifying: I think that all of us, in greater or lesser measure, are in need of purification. Jesus' gaze purifies us, thus making us capable of living with God, of living with the Saints, and above all [sic] of living in communion with those dear to us who have preceded us.[62]

Before considering Benedict's answer, the translation requires correction. At present, the translation has it that in extending to "the very borders of the human being," Jesus's soul goes to a place: "into the *lost places*, to *where* all who *do not arrive* at their life's goal go." But besides a difference in tense, Benedict's original states that Jesus's soul goes to persons: "it goes to the *lost*, to *all those* who *have not arrived* at the goal of their life [*va ai perduti, va a tutti quanti non sono arrivati alla meta della loro vita*]."[63] Moreover, it goes there "in this sense," that it "extends to the *ultimi confini* of the human being," that is, to the ultimate limits. Although *confini* can be translated "borders" in geographical contexts (and Benedict's mention of "a geographical or spatial trip" may have been in the translator's mind — despite the fact that Benedict says such a trip is *not* what the descent was), *limits* seems more relevant in English in the context of the immaterial soul. (We might even allow the English play on words, *final frontier*.)

Benedict opens by referring to the descent as a journey of a soul. Which soul? One always united to the Father but also one that, at its limits, was united *in that way* with those who are lost, the lost being "those who have not arrived" at their life's goal. Consistent with what he has said as a private person, Benedict's insistence that Jesus's soul "is always in contact with the Father" reiterates his focus on the humanity of Christ in relation to the descent and his view that there is no real abandonment by the Father.

What, then, are the "limits" where His soul finds itself? Benedict's text does not specify. It is unclear what it means for Christ's human soul to extend to these ultimate limits of the human being. Consistency with his earlier work, including *Spe salvi* and *Jesus of Nazareth*, could suggest he means that

62. "Seven Questions for the Pope," Catholic News Service (April 22, 2011).

63. "Intervista a Benedetto XVI Trasmessa in Italia nel Programma di Rai Uno 'A Sua Immagine. Domande su Gesù'" (April 22, 2011).

Jesus's experience of the temptation to sin in the face of approaching death and His suffering on the cross unite him to those in anguish.

However, Benedict does not here identify such an experience. Moreover, those earlier treatments focused on Christ before His death, whereas given the context of the question put to the pope, it does appear Benedict is asserting something concrete about Jesus's experience after death for the first time among the readily available public texts. His going to these "limits" may then be intended to refer to Christ's undergoing the full range of human existence.[64] Just as He accepted death, even the death of the cross, He took upon Himself what follows. As Christ had a real human soul, He could experience the most dramatic state of human existence, that of the separated soul. Thus His soul went to the realm of the dead, where there were already individuals from the past who had preceded Him. In this way His "descent . . . into the depth of the human being" is also a "descent . . . into humanity's past."

Besides consistency with the context, this second reading, in which the "ultimate limits" refer to the state of the separated soul, is preferable because it is consistent with past expositions. From the beginning, wherever Ratzinger alluded to Christ after His death and before His resurrection (that is, in the condition of the separated soul), he emphasized Christ's transformative effect upon death and this without asserting that Christ Himself suffered after death. This same time frame seems indicated when Benedict similarly says here that Christ gives access to heaven (the transformative effect) and is Himself always united to the Father. It is also suggested when Benedict stresses how the effectiveness of the redemption reaches in a different way those who live and die after Christ's descent. (This latter emphasis also indicates that, since Christ's work among the souls from the past is completed in His descent, when Benedict mentions those who "have not" arrived at their life's goal, he is really referring to those who "had not" then yet arrived there.)

So how does Benedict continue with regard to the descent itself? Consistent with the *Catechism of the Catholic Church* (#634), he emphasizes that the descent article is significant for showing that salvation in Christ reaches into the ages before the Incarnation. And consistent with his earlier pontifical texts, he characterizes the Fathers as speaking with the "image" of Jesus taking Adam and Eve by the hand. What is new is that Benedict passes from this image to — at long last — the event of the descent itself: *it is by taking Adam and Eve by the hand that Christ creates access to heaven and God.*

64. Compare John Paul II's catechesis on the descent in his General Audience (January 11, 1989), #1.

Benedict's new move is highly significant, because only a reality can bring about a reality; a metaphor or an image cannot cause a real event. Thus if the effect (there being access to heaven) is real, the cause (Christ's taking hold of Adam and Eve) must likewise be. If heaven is to be opened, there must be a real action that causes it to be so, and if it is opened to someone by someone, those persons must be real.

Thus, if the real efficacy of the redemption "embraces the past," it must affect real individual persons of the past. To speak about the past is a way to speak of the realities of that time. Hence the Fathers, speaking of Adam and Eve, mean our first parents as individuals and not just human beings in general. (And since we don't have birth certificates for them, let's call them Adam and Eve . . .) Indeed, if as Benedict says, those individuals stand for humanity as a whole, they do so in virtue of being the primogenitors of the human race.

So, while it is accurate to say "taking by the hand" is an image when used with respect to disembodied souls, it would be a mistake to go on to conclude that Jesus drawing specific persons who lived in the past to perfect communion with God in the realm of the dead is merely an image. The fact that separated souls have no hands does not mean to take such a soul "by the hand" is a meaningless statement. It is a metaphor to represent the real union such a soul can have, namely, a spiritual union. This unifying event must be real and must occur in the realm of the dead because Benedict stresses that the descent reaches men and women of the past, and those men and women are both real and dead. Again, if this effect of union with God is real, it means real men and women were united to Him by a real cause, namely, Christ in His descent. Only a reality can bring about a reality.

A question arises whether those granted access to God in Christ's descent are all the dead, or only some. Was the entire netherworld emptied? On the one hand, it would seem all the dead are granted heaven if "Adam and Eve" are taken, not as particular individuals, but as a corporate term for all humanity. And this Benedict seems to do in his interpretation of the Church Fathers and in saying that "the Redemption . . . embraces the past, all men and women of all time."

However, this conclusion would overlook that it is precisely the redemption in Christ that reaches into the past. If *that* is to reach the past, it must do so in its fundamental characteristics. If one of these is that union with God by grace at least at the time of a person's death is what justifies him, making him an heir of heaven, then that intrinsic requirement applied also to the people of the past, even if the means by which God communicates His grace to humanity have varied over time. The parable of Lazarus and the rich man (Lk 16:19-31), for example, makes clear that a fundamental change in one's relationship with God is impossible after death. So those individuals united to God in Christ's descent had died united to Him by grace. Consequently, it seems best to take Benedict's references to "humanity" as indefinite; that is, with Christ's descent, heaven is now open, theoretically to all, but not necessarily all enter, because that depends on their response to God during their earthly life. The parables of the invitation to the wedding banquet (Mt 22:1-14; Lk 14:16-24) are also relevant here. In the image of Christ grasping the dead by the hand to guide them on high, the dead must also let themselves be grasped and led by God, and their doing so after death directly reflects whether they did so in life.

The upshot is that, if what the *Catechism* and Benedict have said about the descent extending the efficacy, or fruit, of the redemption to ages past is fact and true, and so to be believed, then *the traditional doctrine must be fact and true, and so to be believed*: *that Christ in His descent gave full access to God, who is the essence of heaven, to the individual men and women who had lived and died united to Him is exactly the traditional doctrine!* Christ's doing so is how He brings communion into the realm of death, the thing Ratzinger/Benedict has most consistently emphasized in his discussions of the descent.

* * *

As we have seen in our examination of Ratzinger/Benedict's theology of Christ's descent into hell in chapters 2 and 3, Ratzinger never asserts, as Balthasar does, that the redemption was incomplete upon the Cross, that Christ's suffering intensified after His death into abandonment in His filial relationship to the Father, that He was literally made sin in His descent, and that the whole Trinity experienced that event. On the contrary, Ratzinger was explicit that he "[found] it difficult fully to concur" with Balthasar's theology of Holy Saturday. His lack of agreement with Balthasar's most essential theses makes it difficult to see where he concurred with him at all.

Ratzinger's insistence that the living cannot know what it is to experience the state of death makes him reluctant, unlike Balthasar, to assert much about Christ after His death. Consequently, some of Ratzinger's early treatments focus instead on the loneliness of dying. In this way, Christ's "descent" becomes the approach to death and any suffering in that "descent" is firmly located during the closing hours of His life. Ratzinger specifies the lonely and anguished (though in Christ's case, also trusting) psychological character of such a descent to the gates of death, but not that of the descent beyond them. Where he does hazard characterizing the state after death also as loneliness, it is as the common human fate that Christ transforms by His own being dead, because He Himself is communion between God and man. More recently, in *Jesus of Nazareth*, Ratzinger has stressed that Christ struggled with the temptations we experience in this life and suffered human anguish, transforming and redeeming these through His trust and obedience, particularly in Gethsemane and His final word of self-commitment from the cross before His death. Unambiguously, Ratzinger considers the descent, whether before or after death, a source of consolation and encouragement for human and Christian struggles with suffering and death. In short, without specifying concretely what happened after Christ's death, Ratzinger emphasizes the significance to the living of Christ having died.

Continuity and contrast are found in Benedict's papal works: while he initially handled the descent cautiously, as metaphor and image, his approach grew increasingly concrete. In his 2011 television interview he drew the closest yet to an explicit statement about the nature of Christ's descent after death, and this in a way that indirectly but necessarily espouses the traditional doctrine.

With respect to our comparison of Balthasar, Ratzinger/Benedict XVI, and John Paul II, the point is worth underscoring: their friendship notwithstanding, Ratzinger's theology of Christ's descent into hell has always differed substantially in content from Balthasar's, developing to the point that Benedict most recently essentially affirmed the traditional doctrine.

Table 3. *Ratzinger on Christ's Descent after His Election as Benedict XVI*

Jesus of Nazareth, vol. 1 (2007)	The "descent" is Christ's human experience of temptation, which He accepts in virtue of His baptism. Experience of temptation is described as a sort of "descent into hell," but beyond being an event involving some element of danger, the significance remains unclear because it is not specified what the descent is. Other references are similarly too ambiguous to be conclusive.
Jesus of Nazareth, vol. 2 (2011)	Christ's descent is not discussed. Ps 22 is treated differently than before: it is interpreted as a prayer of corporate personality rather than an expression of Christ's individual situation. Christ's fear and anguish are discussed in connection with Gethsemane instead of the cross. Balthasarian language about Christ's union with sin is used to convey instead Christ's experience of temptation. Christ's obedience in the face of this temptation is His high priestly sacrifice that, as such, draws His human brethren into His righteousness. The whole Christ is definitively preserved from corruption during the time His body is buried.

Table 4. *Benedict XVI on Christ's Descent*

Visit to Auschwitz address (May 28, 2006)	Benedict uses *hell* metaphorically for suffering in earthly life.
Spe salvi (November 30, 2007), #37	He draws upon a martyr's letter and then Ps 138(139). He does not reference *gli inferi* [abode of the dead] of the creed, but rather *l'inferno* [hell of damnation]. He uses *hell* [*l'inferno*] metaphorically for suffering in earthly life.

Easter Vigil Homily, 2007	He draws upon Ps 138(139), Ps 23(24), and the Easter icons. Ratzinger's themes of silence, loneliness, and apparent abandonment are not present. Still present is that Christ brings God's communion with Him beyond death. It is ambiguous whether the saving effect of Christ's descent extends to all the dead, all humanity, or only to some. Similar to Ratzinger's use of metaphors, Benedict treats his descriptions of Christ's descent as "imagery." Hence, also similar to Ratzinger, Benedict focuses on the significance of the descent (whatever it was) for Christians rather than on what happened to Christ. He connects baptism to death, with Christ present to us on both sides.
"Veneration of the Holy Shroud Meditation" (May 2, 2010)	He calls the Shroud "the Icon of Holy Saturday," and also draws upon the homily that is part of the Divine Office for that day. God's hiddenness in the silence of Holy Saturday has two facets: His death in the flesh and His transformation of the realm of the dead. Christ's death is in the flesh, not in His divinity (as Balthasar would also have it). The facet of Christ's death highlights the living's existential sense of interior void (see similar themes in Ratzinger's first "Meditation on Holy Week"). Christ transforms the realm of death, and perhaps also the event of death, by His entrance as love, light, and communion. Benedict says he will talk about what happened to Christ, but instead remains focused on the significance of the descent for the living.
June 11, 2010, homily; and *Verbum Domini* (September 30, 2010)	Benedict uses *hell* metaphorically for suffering in earthly life.
"In His Image" Italian television interview (April 22, 2011)	Points of continuity with his earlier papal and private work include the following: the descent is a journey of soul (hence, in Christ's humanity); there is no real abandonment by the Father; and reference is made to patristic "imagery." For the first time, what occurred to Christ after death is specified, and it is the traditional doctrine: in His descent, Christ gives full access to God to the individual men and women who had let themselves be united to Christ.

General Audience (February 8, 2012)	He implicitly confirms that *Spe salvi*, #37 refers to earthly suffering.

Table 5. *Differences between Balthasar and Ratzinger on Christ's Descent after Ratzinger's Election as Benedict XVI*

Balthasar	**Ratzinger (after His Election)**	**Benedict (Early)**	**Benedict (Most Recently)**
Christ's descent occurs *after death.*	Christ's "descent" occurs *before death.*	Christ's "descent" occurs *before death.*	Christ's descent occurs *after death.*
Christ's abandonment by God is *real.*	Abandonment is not a particular theme.	Abandonment is not a particular theme.	Abandonment is not a particular theme, but Christ *remains always "in contact with" the Father* (so any abandonment could only be apparent).
Christ descends in virtue of His *divinity.*	Christ "descends" in virtue of His *humanity.*	Christ "descends" in virtue of His *humanity.*	Christ descends in virtue of His *humanity.*
Christ descends to *Sheol in Balthasar's sense.*	Christ "descends" into *the danger of temptation.*	Christ "descends" into *earthly sufferings.*	Christ descends to *men and women of the past.*
Christ suffers *union with, and punishment for, all sin.*	Christ suffers *human anguish and temptation.*	Christ undergoes *sufferings of earthly life.*	No clear indication that Christ suffers.

Balthasar	**Ratzinger (after His Election)**	**Benedict (Early)**	**Benedict (Most Recently)**
Christ *undergoes alienation* in the abode of the dead.	Christ *brings His own communion* into the abode of the dead, and *is preserved from all corruption* during the time His body is buried.	Christ *brings His own communion* into the abode of the dead.	Christ *unites with God the individual men and women of the past who had let themselves be united to Him.*
The Incarnation is *suspended* in the descent.	The Incarnation remains *intact* in the "descent" and after death.	The Incarnation remains *intact* in the "descent" and after death.	The Incarnation remains *intact* in the descent after death.

4

JOHN PAUL II ON THE DESCENT

What exactly did happen in Christ's descent, if not what Balthasar suggests? In the previous two chapters, we saw how Ratzinger both said he could not agree with Balthasar and hesitated to assert what happened to Christ after His death, while Benedict has approached that event only obliquely. Perhaps Benedict sees his admired predecessor's teaching as providing the context that would make his own allusions plain, since John Paul II was explicit. John Paul II's clarity and precision on this topic makes his beliefs about Christ's descent easy to see. In consequence, exposition of his theology can proceed more directly and will be shorter than our discussion of Ratzinger/Benedict. In this chapter, we will also consider what the universal catechism promulgated by John Paul II, the *Catechism of the Catholic Church*, says about Christ's descent, together with its similarly universal predecessor, the *Roman Catechism* (also known as the *Catechism of the Council of Trent*, since it was promulgated after that Council for use in the entire Church).

Catechesis on Christ's Descent (January 11, 1989, Audience)

John Paul II discussed Christ's descent most extensively in his general audience of January 11, 1989, just six months after Balthasar's death. John Paul II systematically gave catecheses on the creed in his general audiences over an extended period of time (1985-96). It is helpful for the purposes of our comparison that John Paul II engages this topic at a time after Balthasar's theology had reached the most developed form it would take. John Paul II concludes this audience with the following summary:

> [T]he truth expressed by the Apostles' Creed in the words "he descended into hell," while confirming the reality of Christ's death, at the same time proclaims the beginning of his glorification and not only of his glorification but of all those who by means of his redemptive sacrifice, have been prepared for the sharing in his glory in the happiness of God's kingdom.[1]

Here John Paul II says the truth — not the metaphor or image, but the truth — of the article is threefold: Christ truly died; His resulting descent initiates his glorification; and in His descent, Christ extended his beatitude to the souls of those awaiting Him, which the living who likewise remain united to Him will also eventually share. A closer look at all three points will show significant contrasts with Balthasar's theology.

Regarding the first point, John Paul II had explained earlier in his audience what death means here:

> During the three (incomplete) days between the moment when he 'expired' (cf. Mk 15:37) and the resurrection, Jesus experienced the 'state of death', that is, the separation of body and soul, as in the case of all people. This is the [first] meaning of the words 'he descended into hell'.[2]

The article "is a confirmation that this was a real, and not merely an apparent, death. His soul, separated from the body, was glorified in God, but his body lay in the tomb as a corpse."[3] Hence John Paul II is also explicit that the descent occurs "after [Christ's] death on the cross."[4] Although death as separation of body and soul has been accused of being a Hellenistic corruption of the biblical witness, it is, in fact, wholly consistent with biblical anthropology.[5] (For one, God's people of the Old Testament venerated the

1. John Paul II, General Audience (January 11, 1989), #8, translation of the *L'Osservatore Romano Weekly Edition in English* (January 16, 1989): 1, 16. Italics not in the original Italian version on the Vatican website have been removed.

2. John Paul II, General Audience (January 11, 1989), #4. The English translation gives "primary" for the Italian *primo*, which is more accurately translated "first."

3. John Paul II, General Audience (January 11, 1989), #4.

4. John Paul II, General Audience (January 11, 1989), #4.

5. C. Spicq, "La Révélation de l'Enfer dans la Sainte Écriture," in *L'Enfer*, Foi Vivante

tombs of the patriarchs even as they spoke of sheol, a practice that indicates an understanding of those two principles of the human person we call *body* and *soul.*) John Paul II presumes such consistency, couching his treatment of the descent in a thoroughly scriptural context and, in essence, describing it as a biblical theology.[6]

In contrast to the lengths to which Balthasar must go to characterize Christ's "state of death" as a suspension of the Incarnation that makes possible a union with sin-in-itself (the *visio mortis*), John Paul II has no need to defend his straightforward understanding of death, relying on common human experience of the difference between a corpse and a living person, as well as on common Christian theological elements that are well established in Church teaching. The Fourth Lateran Council (1215), for example, specifies that Christ descended "in soul" (DS 801), and the *Catechism of the Catholic Church* (#366) matter-of-factly treats death as the separation of body and soul.

John Paul II's second point about the truth of the article is that Christ's descent begins his glorification. Balthasar would understand the descent's glory as the perfect manifestation of the divine love of the Trinity as the Son, united to what is most ungodly, experiences in His filial relationship the Father's wrath while being unconsciously united to Him by the Holy Spirit. That, however, is not what John Paul II means by *glorification.* On the contrary, John Paul II describes it as Christ's soul being "glorified in God,"[7] "the heavenly glorification of his soul from the very moment of his death,"[8] being "alive in the spirit,"[9] "glorified in his soul,"[10] and "admitted to the fullness of the beatific vision of God."[11] In other words, John Paul II understands Christ's human soul to be newly glorified in His descent and this

---

52 (Paris: Les Éditions de la Revue des Jeunes, 1950), 93, 105-6, 108. See also Heinz-Jürgen Vogels, *Christi Abstieg ins Totenreich und das Läuterungsgericht an den Toten*, Freiburger Theologische Studien 120. Band (Freiburg: Herder, 1976), 106-7. Passages such as Gen 2:7 and Ezek 37:6, 8 provide a basis within biblical culture for an anthropological distinction similar to the "Greek" one.

6. John Paul II, General Audience (January 11, 1989), #3: "There are numerous New Testament texts from which the formula ["He descended into hell"] is derived"; see also #4.

7. John Paul II, General Audience (January 11, 1989), #4.

8. John Paul II, General Audience (January 11, 1989), #5. See also his General Audience of December 7, 1988, ##6-7. The paragraphs in the English translation of the 1988 audience are unnumbered; the paragraph numbers given refer to those in the Italian original.

9. John Paul II, General Audience (January 11, 1989), #5.

10. John Paul II, General Audience (January 11, 1989), #6.

11. John Paul II, General Audience (January 11, 1989), #6. Compare the General Audience of December 7, 1988, #7.

in a way that entails the fullness of spiritual life. In contrast, Balthasar sees the "glorification" of the Son occurring in His filial relation to the Father and this through the spiritual death of union with sin and abandonment by God.

John Paul II's precision that the descent begins Christ's glorification with that of His entire soul follows the traditional belief that Christ had the beatific vision throughout His entire human life. Just as possessing the beatific vision before death was unique to Him as the God-man, the manner in which it affected Him was unique: before His death, it did not prevent Him from experiencing human suffering. (John Paul II also articulates this position in *Novo Millennio Ineunte*, ##26-27.) After Christ's death, however, He suffered no more; His entire soul rejoiced in God. Hence also, John Paul II carefully says Christ was "admitted to the *fullness* of the beatific vision of God," and not simply that He was "admitted to the beatific vision," because the latter could suggest He had not had it before. John Paul II's precision about the glorification of Christ's soul in His descent is also entirely consistent with his characterization of Christ's resurrection as "his true glorification"[12] in another audience: "The *crowning* point of the paschal mystery"[13] is the event of Easter Sunday, because then the *whole* Christ, body and soul, is glorified, whereas in His descent, it is only His entire *soul* that is glorified.

Not only would a Balthasarian reading of John Paul II's catechesis on the descent have to overlook John Paul II's insistence on Christ's soul and the full extent of His possession of the beatific vision, it would also have to neglect what John Paul II says about the word *hell*: "It should also be mentioned straight-away that the word 'hell' does not mean the hell of eternal damnation, but the abode of the dead which is 'sheol' in Hebrew and 'hades' in Greek (cf. Acts 2:31)."[14] It is an historical fact that *hell* (and its equivalent in other languages) used to have a broader meaning in Christian contexts than it does today, and it was within that broader context that the doctrine of Christ's descent developed. Thus, to assume *hell* in the creed means the place of eternal punishment (*gehenna*) as it does today is a simple, but serious, error. Aware both of what the Christian profession means and of the potential for misunderstanding, John Paul II here *contrasts* damnation with sheol; that is, the sheol to which Christ descended is not the abode of the

12. John Paul II, General Audience (November 30, 1988), #6. The paragraphs in the English translation of the 1988 audience are unnumbered; the paragraph numbers given refer to those in the Italian original.

13. John Paul II, General Audience (December 7, 1988), #5, emphasis added.

14. John Paul II, General Audience (January 11, 1989), #2.

damned. While a Balthasarian may say, "Yes, as I understand it, Sheol is worse than the hell of eternal damnation," the burden of proof would be on him to show that *John Paul II* meant it that way.

It will be difficult going. For, "As dead — and *at the same time* as alive 'forevermore' — Christ has the keys of death and Hades (cf. Rev 1:17-18)."[15] John Paul II's application of this eschatological verse to Christ's historical descent is significant: on Holy Saturday, Christ is glorified as He will be universally manifested to be at the end times. A similar, though less explicitly worded, parallelism is seen later in John Paul II's **General Audience of April 3, 1996.** There he describes the Easter Vigil as simultaneously celebration of the "'new exodus' to the promised land" (i.e., the opening of heaven), commemoration of Jesus's resurrection, and vigil for His second coming "when Easter will reach its fulfillment."[16] In other words, he highlights that Christ's glorification unites these three mysteries: He is first glorified in the eyes of the dead during His descent, then in the eyes of the Church on earth at His resurrection, and finally in the eyes of all at His return.

All Balthasarian gymnastic interpretation of John Paul II is ruled out by his third point, however: commenting on 1 Pet 3:19, John Paul II says the verse, through the metaphor of the preaching to the souls in prison, indicates the — note: non-metaphorical — "extension of *Christ's* salvation to the *just men and women* who had died before him."[17] He "communicates *his state of beatitude* to *all the just* whose state of death he shares in regard *to the body.*"[18] Two elements are contrary to Balthasar here: First, far from Christ undergoing God-abandonment or any suffering during His descent, John Paul II carefully indicates that the others' beatitude flows from Christ, who possesses it first. He is like them in being dead according to the body; He is unlike them in that He rejoices in the fullness of the beatific vision immediately upon His descent and is the source of it for the just awaiting Him. It is precisely in this way that "the souls of the just" are freed[19]: "*Through Christ* and *in Christ* there opens up before them the definitive freedom of the life of the Spirit, as a participation in the Life of God."[20]

Second, also contrary to Balthasar but with some echo in Ratzinger/

15. John Paul II, General Audience (January 11, 1989), #6, emphasis added.
16. John Paul II, General Audience (April 3, 1996), #3.
17. John Paul II, General Audience (January 11, 1989), #5, emphasis added.
18. John Paul II, General Audience (January 11, 1989), #6, emphasis added.
19. John Paul II, General Audience (January 11, 1989), #6.
20. John Paul II, General Audience (January 11, 1989), #7, emphasis added.

Benedict, Christ is neither abandoned and alone nor companion to all the dead. Instead, he specifically joins the company of the holy dead to share His joy with them. John Paul II reiterates no fewer than five times in his 1989 catechesis on the descent that *it is the just* who benefit from "the extension of redemption to all people of all times and places."[21]

Implicit in the pope's audience is a distinction between a very precise use of the words *redemption* and *salvation*, or between what are technically called *the objective redemption* and *the subjective redemption*: the first is what Christ did for us; the second is the beatific union with God of those in whom Christ's work bore fruit during their lives. Hence John Paul II says that in Christ's freeing of the just is

> *put into effect* the salvific power of Christ's sacrificial death which brought redemption to all, even to those who died before his coming and his 'descent into hell', but who [had been] contacted by his justifying grace.[22]

In other words, the fact that Christ redeemed all does not necessarily mean that all are saved. Christ's death redeemed everyone (that is, atoned for everyone's sins), thus making salvation possible for all. However, that effect (salvation) can become definitively actualized only in those who are renewed by grace, and that was true of some who died before Him. (There is nothing to prevent God, knowing the redemption to come, from giving grace in virtue of it to those who lived before Christ's crucifixion, and Scripture gives ample evidence of this being the case in, for example, God's relationship to the patriarchs and prophets.) Thus, having completed redemption in the blood of His cross, Christ gave salvation, gave beatitude, to the holy dead in His descent.

This view contrasts with Balthasar's. For him, Christ's descent into hell is timeless so He is somehow suffering there with all who have or will be damned, His embrace of an abandonment worse than theirs out of love for them continually working to soften their resistance to God's love.[23] In other

21. John Paul II, General Audience (January 11, 1989), #7; references to the souls of the just are in ##5-7.

22. John Paul II, General Audience (January 11, 1989), #6, emphasis added; brackets indicate correction to the translation, which has "were" instead of "had been" (Ital. *furono*).

23. For discussion and references, see Alyssa Lyra Pitstick, *Light in Darkness: Hans Urs von Balthasar and the Catholic Doctrine of Christ's Descent into Hell* (Grand Rapids: Eerdmans, 2007), 265-68. One example would be Balthasar, "On Vicarious Representation," *Spirit*

words, for Balthasar, Christ descends not only to the just of the past, but to the unjust of all time, perhaps even making possible the conversion after death of those in hell.

Easter Vigil Homily (1986)

Although stated less explicitly, the same points in John Paul II's 1989 catechesis that contrast with Balthasar's positions had also been made earlier in John Paul II's homily for Easter Vigil, 1986, in connection to the word *pasch* (as in *paschal mystery*):

> ... *Mors, ero mors tua* [Death, I will be your death; Hos 13:14].
>
> Thus says he who is our Pasch.
>
> Pasch means "passage". It is the passage toward life through death, just as, under the Old Covenant, Israel once passed toward life through the death of the paschal lamb. Nevertheless, that was only a passage toward another life upon this earth: from the slavery of Egypt toward the freedom in the promised land.
>
> The Church's Pasch signifies the passage toward the eternal life that comes from God, that is life in God.[24]

In other words, Christ is the one through whom those who were called by God and who followed His will pass to eternal life in God.

The eternal life signified here cannot be limited to the life of the resurrected body as manifested on Easter morning and as will occur at the end of time. For then one would exclude from eternal life all the saints who have not yet been resurrected bodily, and precisely the opposite was dogmatically defined in 1336 by Pope Benedict XII in the Constitution *Benedictus Deus* (*On the Beatific Vision of God*):

---

and Institution, Explorations in Theology, vol. 4, trans. Edward T. Oakes (San Francisco: Ignatius, 1995), 422: On Holy Saturday, Jesus "is dead with the dead (but out of a final love). But this is precisely how he disturbs the absolute loneliness that the sinner strives for: the sinner who wants to be 'damned' by God now rediscovers God in his loneliness — but this time he rediscovers God in the absolute impotence of love. For now God has placed himself in solidarity with those who have damned themselves, entering into nontime in a way we could never anticipate."

24. John Paul II, Omelia (March 29, 1986), ##2-3.

> *Since the passion and death* of the Lord Jesus Christ, *these souls* [those of "the saints" who "were not in need of any purification when they died . . . or else, if they then needed . . . some purification, after they have been purified after death," including "the souls of all the saints who departed from this world *before* the passion of our Lord Jesus Christ"] *have seen and see the divine essence* with an intuitive vision and even face to face . . . ; and in this vision they enjoy the divine essence. Moreover, *by this vision and enjoyment* the souls of those who have already died are *truly blessed and have eternal life* and rest.[25]

Although *Benedictus Deus* is typically remembered for defining the immediacy of recompense for those who die after Christ, it actually defines the timing of reward or punishment for all, including those who died before Christ. Hence it also specifies *as part of the dogmatic definition* that, after Christ's death on the cross, the souls then ready for heaven received the beatific vision. Consequently, the Church's first *pasch*, the first such passage through death to eternal life, is the passage of the souls of the holy dead into the fullness of God's life, the essential glory of heaven, through Christ present among them in the realm of the dead. He is their, and our, *pasch*.

Moreover, it is specifically in virtue of Christ's death on the cross and united to it that anyone makes that passage. Contrary to Balthasar, for whom redemption only reaches completion in Sheol, John Paul II says that "the Pasch of Christ was fulfilled *upon this earth. On this earth*, death was destroyed by death."[26] Since sin was the cause of death, through Christ's obedience unto death and in His passing to perfection of human life in and through death, He destroyed sin's heritage, including for those who had already died.[27] "He visited them with the power of his death: with the redemptive power of his death. With the life-giving power of his death. *O mors, ero mors tua!*"[28] He was the death of death by living and dying in the sinlessness of His obedient love, by giving life to the dead in the realm of death, and then by becoming the firstborn of all mortals in His resurrection. His death continues to be the death of death in that the living are "'through baptism indeed buried with him in death, so that as Christ was raised from the dead

25. Jacques Dupuis, ed., *The Christian Faith in the Doctrinal Documents of the Catholic Church*, 6th ed. (Staten Island, NY: Alba House, 1996), #2305 (DS 1000), emphasis added.

26. John Paul II, Omelia (March 29, 1986), #4, emphasis added.

27. John Paul II, Omelia (March 29, 1986), ##5-6.

28. John Paul II, Omelia (March 29, 1986), #6.

by the glory of the Father, we too might walk in the new life' (Rom 6:4)."[29] In the previous chapter (pp. 43-45), we saw how this theme of the redemptive impact of Christ's obedience appears also in John Paul II's October 19, 1988, audience and is echoed in volume 2 of Ratzinger's *Jesus of Nazareth*.

Audience (June 20, 2001)

In his 1989 audience, John Paul II states that he is talking about the truth of the descent, about what really happened, about what Scripture reveals, about what the faith of the Catholic Church has been and is. He is addressing the Church at large with the language of faith common to the Church, not with code language unique to one theologian and his school. That his meaning in the 1989 audience is straightforward is indisputably confirmed by his audience of June 20, 2001.

There, John Paul II describes how the triumphal entrance verses of Psalm 23(24) are "applied by the Christian liturgy of the East and the West to the victorious Descent of Christ to the Limbo of the Fathers . . . and to the Risen Lord's Ascension into heaven."[30] The liturgy is a public profession of the Church's faith, a fact distilled in the ancient principle, *lex orandi, lex credendi*: the law of prayer is the law of belief. Here, John Paul II emphasizes that the liturgy of the *universal* Church (the "liturgy of the East and the West") applies the psalm of the king's triumphal taking possession of part of his domain to Christ's descent not to Balthasar's Sheol or Ratzinger's state of psychological anxiety or even death as an event or some ambiguous resultant state, but to the limbo of the Fathers.

That abode of the dead, explains the *Roman Catechism* (RC), is where

> the souls of the just before the coming of Christ the Lord, were received, and where, without experiencing any sort of pain, but supported by the blessed hope of redemption, they enjoyed peaceful repose.[31]

Hell has a broad sense, as mentioned earlier, and it can mean any non-heavenly part of the after-life. The limbo of the Fathers, though not a part of heaven, was hardly the heart of hell. This characteristic is conveyed by its

29. John Paul II, Omelia (March 29, 1986), #7.
30. John Paul II, General Audience (June 20, 2001), #5.
31. *Catechism of the Council of Trent*, 63.

name, *limbo*, from the Latin, *limbus*, meaning *edge* or *border*. The "fathers" of this limbo are the biblical patriarchs and, the whole being named by the part, all those "souls of the just" who died before Christ.

John Paul II's explicit parallelism in this audience underscores that Christ's descent to the limbo of the Fathers is as real, as historical, and as victorious as His ascension to heaven. It is not that one is a mere image or metaphor, and the other is real; that one is a victory concealed in suffering, the other a victory manifest in splendor. Instead, both are real and manifestly triumphant.

Catechism of the Catholic Church (1997)

John Paul II promulgated the contemporary *Catechism of the Catholic Church* (CCC) in its finalized version in 1997. The CCC is consistent on several points with earlier expressions of the Church's doctrine of Christ's descent, including John Paul II's catechesis and the *Roman Cathechism* (RC). (Is it just coincidence that Ratzinger expressed his continued inability to concur with Balthasar in his introduction for *The Sabbath of History* the same year the CCC came out?)

The first point of consistency in the CCC is that "the [descent's] first meaning" is "that Jesus, like all men, experienced death and in his soul joined the others in the realm of the dead" (#632). So Christ's death was like others' in being the separation of body and soul, rather than being some archetypal spiritual death of union with sin, as Balthasar has it. The CCC's definition of death as the body and soul separating is explicit in an earlier paragraph (#366) and is also confirmed by the paragraphs on Christ's burial (##625, 626, 630). The CCC's predecessor, the RC, similarly affirms that when we profess that Jesus died, "we mean that His soul was disunited from His body."[32] Both say that nonetheless God the Son always remained united to His body and soul even when they were separated from each other.[33] So it is true to profess that the Son of God both descended (in soul) and was buried (in body).

However, contrary to Balthasar's view that the Son suffered in His divine filial relation in Sheol, the RC and John Paul II hold that Christ suffered only

32. *Catechism of the Council of Trent*, 53.

33. *Catechism of the Council of Trent*, 53, 62; *Catechism of the Catholic Church* (New Hope, KY: Urbi et Orbi Communications, 1994), ##626, 630.

in His human nature and only before His death. The RC makes clear that "burial, Passion, and also death, apply to Christ Jesus not as God but as man," because "to suffer and die [pertain] to human nature only."[34] The RC is also explicit that Jesus did not suffer in His descent.[35] In his general audience of October 19, 1988, John Paul II similarly stressed that Christ did not suffer in His divine nature, but only in His human one. Given what John Paul II says in his catechesis on the descent about the glorification of Christ's entire soul, such suffering only occurred before His death.

The CCC, RC, and John Paul II thus affirm that Christ's death and descent followed the common human lot because He is truly human. At the same time, His death and descent were shaped by the fact that He is truly divine and sinless. Specifically, as the CCC says, Christ's descent was unique in that "he descended there as Savior, proclaiming the Good News to the spirits imprisoned there."[36] The RC elaborates further:

> [Other men] descended as captives; He as free and victorious among the dead, to subdue those demons by whom, in consequence of guilt, they were held in captivity. Furthermore all others descended, either to endure the most acute torments, or, if exempt from other pain, to be deprived of the vision of God, and to be tortured by the delay of the glory and happiness for which they yearned; Christ the Lord descended, on the contrary, not to suffer, but to liberate the holy and the just from their painful captivity, and to impart to them the fruit of His Passion.[37]

John Paul II had likewise said that the just were freed through Christ communicating to them the salvific effects ("the fruit," RC) of His redemptive death.

Yet another point of consistency in the CCC concerns the abode of the dead to which Christ descended. The CCC, like John Paul II, specifies that it was sheol or hades, and, like the RC, calls it by yet another scriptural name, *Abraham's bosom* (#633). Since the RC also names it the limbo of the Fathers, all four terms refer to the same abode.

Regarding the nature of that abode, both universal catechisms and John

34. *Catechism of the Council of Trent*, 55-56; see also 62.

35. *Catechism of the Council of Trent*, 64.

36. *Catechism of the Catholic Church*, #632. See also *Catechism of the Council of Trent*, 65-65, and John Paul II, General Audience (January 11, 1989), #5.

37. *Catechism of the Council of Trent*, 64. On Jesus being "free and victorious among the dead," see Ps 87:6 in the Vulgate.

Paul II hold that those who were there did not have the vision of God. However, the lack of such vision is "the case for all the dead, whether evil or righteous, while they await the redeemer."[38] The implication is that after the Redeemer's descent, some at least will have that blessed vision — which, as we saw earlier (p. 66), was dogmatically defined in 1336 in *Benedictus Deus*.

Nonetheless, even though no one, just or unjust, had the beatific vision before the Redeemer's descent, there was still a difference among the dead. The CCC (#633) draws upon Christ's parable of Lazarus and the rich man to make this point; it had also been made earlier by the RC in some detail in its distinction among *gehenna* (the hell of eternal punishment), purgatory, and Abraham's bosom.[39] This teaching of the universal catechisms raises an additional difficulty for Balthasar's theology, for he held that there was no such differentiation in the afterlife before Christ's descent.[40]

In drawing upon Christ's parable of Lazarus in Abraham's bosom to name and characterize the abode to which Christ descended, both catechisms imply that the souls there were not suffering, except if by analogy we want to name eager waiting for a delayed loved one and the lack of freedom to go to him "suffering." This extended sense of "suffering" reconciles the RC's description of the limbo of the Fathers as an abode both where the souls of the just were "tortured by the delay of the glory and happiness for which they yearned . . . [in] painful captivity,"[41] and yet also where, "without experiencing any sort of pain, but supported by the blessed hope of redemption, they enjoyed peaceful repose."[42] The catechisms' teaching thus differs also from characterizations of sheol based only upon Old Testament texts that suggest those in the abode of the dead had a shadowy and gloomy existence; Ratzinger's theology showed this sort of tendency in its characterization of death as loneliness, loss of communication, and so on (to the extent that he had the state of the separated soul in mind rather than the event of death).

Finally, the CCC (#633) makes explicit something that is only implicit in the RC, namely, that, "Jesus did not descend into hell to deliver the damned, nor to destroy the hell of damnation"[43] — apparently already existing,

38. *Catechism of the Catholic Church*, #633. See also *Catechism of the Council of Trent*, 64.

39. *Catechism of the Council of Trent*, 63.

40. See discussion and references in Pitstick, *Light in Darkness*, 94-95.

41. *Catechism of the Council of Trent*, 64.

42. *Catechism of the Council of Trent*, 63.

43. A curious reference in John Paul II's catechesis on the descent may also hint at the same affirmation: In paragraph #7, at a point when he is discussing the entrance of the

contrary to Balthasar, who held it did not exist until after Christ's descent[44] — "but to free the just who had gone before him."[45] In short, in Christ's descent, "He opened heaven's gates for the just."[46]

* * *

The Catholic doctrine of Christ's descent into hell, as set forth by John Paul II and the two universal catechisms, can be summarized in four points:[47]

1. The sinless human soul of Christ, united to His divine person, descended only to the realm of the dead reserved for the souls of holy individuals, called the limbo of the Fathers.
2. He liberated those holy souls from there by conferring on them the glory of heaven. Having accomplished humanity's redemption in the blood of his cross, Christ distributes the first fruits of his sacrifice.
3. In doing so, his power and authority were made known to all the dead, both good and evil, and to the fallen angels.
4. Because Christ descended in His sinless soul as the all-holy redeemer, His descent was glorious in a way similar to His resurrection, and He did not suffer in His descent.

The third point is not discussed in this book because it does not feature prominently in John Paul II's catechesis on the descent, which is the topic of the chapter, nor in the CCC promulgated by him. It follows, however, as a corollary of the other points they make and is explicitly

---

just into definitive life, John Paul II has the parenthetical citation, "cf. St. Thomas, *Summa theologica* IIIa, q. 52, a. 6." This article addresses the question, "Whether Christ delivered any of the lost from hell?" to which the answer given is no. If this citation is indeed the one John Paul II intended, it expresses the same point as that quoted here from the *Catechism of the Catholic Church.* (One wonders, though, if the original manuscript had a. 5 instead, because that article directly concerns the deliverance of the just, which is what John Paul II is discussing at that particular moment.)

44. See Pitstick, *Light in Darkness,* 257-74.

45. *Catechism of the Catholic Church,* #633.

46. *Catechism of the Catholic Church,* #637.

47. Readers of *First Things,* the journal of religion in the public square, might recognize these four points as the same ones with which I summarized the Church's doctrine in an exchange of articles on Balthasar and Christ's descent into hell in 2006 and 2007. The articles of the exchange are Alyssa Lyra Pitstick and Edward T. Oakes, S.J., "Balthasar, Hell, and Heresy: An Exchange" (December, 2006): 25-32; "More on Balthasar, Hell, and Heresy" (January, 2007): 16-19; and "Responses to 'Balthasar, Hell, and Heresy'" (March, 2007): 5-14.

present in Trent's catechism: besides Christ's liberation of the just, the RC speaks of a second reason for His descent, namely, that "He might proclaim His power and authority, and that 'every knee should bow, of those that are in heaven, on earth, and under the earth.'"[48] In "subdu[ing] those demons by whom, in consequence of guilt, [the souls of the holy dead] were held in captivity,"[49] in freeing the just and so despoiling the strong man, the Son of God assumes in His human nature dominion of the entire underworld.

Ratzinger continually sought after the significance of Christ's descent even as he shied away from asserting much about the event itself. How might John Paul II's concrete catechesis about the descent event provide a foundation for addressing interest in its meaning?

In every case, the significance of a mystery of Christ for living Christians must be based upon what really happened, what Christ really did, since it is as members of His body that Christians participate in His life, death, and resurrection. Hence, for the early Church, *mystery* was not first and foremost something that puzzled or exceeded the human intellect; it was first participation in the life of God, something that exceeded not just the intellect, but the whole of human life itself. Specifically, it was participation in the life of Christ, the God-man, who made possible and modeled what it is to live God's life in the flesh. The sacraments, which were so closely linked to Christ, played an essential role in this re-living, so to speak, of Christ's own life, death, and resurrection.

It is in this context that baptism was linked to His descent. Baptism was passover to life in Christ, the first step in passover to the fullness of that life in heaven. In Christ's descent, the holy dead made that final exodus in His company. In doing so, the souls of the just in the limbo of the Fathers prefigured for the living our union with Christ. Like them, those who are now united to God and justified by His grace, who now believe in Him and keep His commandments, and who now await His return in glory will also someday see Him coming to bring us into His heavenly glory if we persevere in His friendship.

Of course, much more could be said about the theological richness of the descent, its connection to baptism, and its significance for Christian life. Indeed, much more has been said in Christian history. But that is a topic for another book.

48. *Catechism of the Council of Trent*, 65, with interior quotation of Phil 2:10.
49. *Catechism of the Council of Trent*, 64.

Table 6. *Differences between Balthasar and John Paul II on Christ's Descent*

Balthasar	John Paul II
Christ undergoes *both physical and spiritual death.*	Christ undergoes *physical death, the separation of the body and soul.*
Christ descends to *Sheol in Balthasar's sense.*	Christ descends to *the limbo of the Fathers.*
Christ is *really abandoned by God.*	Christ receives *the fullness of the beatific vision.*
Christ descends in virtue of His *divinity.*	Christ descends in virtue of His *human soul.*
Christ suffers *union with, and punishment for, all sin* in His descent.	Christ's *glorification begins with His descent.*
Christ *atones for all sin through His descent.*	Christ's descent is the *beginning of the fruits* of the atonement, completed with His death on the cross.
Christ *undergoes alienation* in the abode of the dead.	Christ *extends His beatitude to the souls of the just,* thereby freeing them from the limbo of the Fathers by giving them heaven's glory.
Christ is present to *the dead of all time, including to the unjust.*	Christ joins *only the just who had died before Him.*
The Incarnation is *suspended* in the descent.	The Incarnation remains *intact* in the descent.

5

A SIGNIFICANT SIDENOTE ON SCHÖNBORN

The common doctrine of Benedict XII (as author of *Benedictus Deus*), the *Roman Catechism* (RC), the *Catechism of the Catholic Church* (CCC), and John Paul II (to name just the two universal catechisms and just two popes) contrasts dramatically with Balthasar's theology of Holy Saturday. It is in light of this contrast that a frequently quoted comment made by then-Auxiliary Bishop of Vienna Christoph Schönborn must be considered. Since Schönborn was general editor of the CCC, what he said about Balthasar in connection to that summary of Catholic doctrine is viewed as significant by Balthasar's supporters. As we shall see in this chapter, Schönborn does indeed shed important light on the nature of the Church's doctrine of the descent and so on how we ought to view John Paul II's, Ratzinger/Benedict XVI's, and Balthasar's theologies of the descent. Consequently, even though the bishop does not appear in the subtitle of this book, it is well worthwhile looking closely at what he had to say.

What Schönborn Said

Schönborn's comment about Balthasar's theology appears in his *Introduction to the* Catechism of the Catholic Church. Before all else, it is important to be absolutely clear that this *Introduction* is not a part of the CCC itself. It is a separate book altogether, and not an official document of the Church. Coauthored by Cardinal Ratzinger and Schönborn, the *Introduction* collects in written form a number of presentations the two gave on the CCC's history and general character (Ratzinger) and its unifying themes (Schönborn). The book's title comes from their goal to provide "elementary aids to reading and study"[1] of the CCC, in other words, to introduce the text.

This goal is readily manifest in one of Schönborn's contributions, "A Short Introduction to the Four Parts of the Catechism," in which he "point[s] out a few aspects which seem[ed] to [him] to be worthy of attention."[2] As he comments on Part One of the CCC, which is structured according to the Apostles' Creed, Schönborn has the following to say about the articles on Christ's Passion, death, descent, and resurrection. (Numbers in parentheses are paragraph numbers in the CCC.)

> d) Belief in Jesus Christ's redemptive act is of the greatest significance for the Christian faith. What the Catechism says with reference to Jesus's trial from a historical point of view (595-96) is shown in the light of revelation to be the fulfillment of God's redemptive design. Jesus's death is first considered in the light of God's salvific plan, which excludes no one (509-605). Christ is not the passive victim of this decree. On the contrary, he offered himself to the Father for our sins (606-9). At the last Supper, he anticipated this self-surrender eucharistically (610-11), before assenting to the Father's will to the very end in Gethsemani (612). That Jesus's death is the perfect sacrifice of the new Covenant, which he offered for all, and that it is an expiatory sacrifice (613-17) are truths of the faith belonging to the original substance of the Christian Creed.
>
> e) The fifth article of faith (*"He descended into hell, on the third day he rose again from the dead"*) concerns an equally central good of the Christian patrimony of faith. The brief paragraph on Jesus's descent into hell keeps to what is the common property of the Church's exegetical tradition. Newer interpretations, such as that of a Hans Urs von Balthasar (the contemplation of Holy Saturday), however profound and helpful they may be, have not yet experienced that reception which would justify their inclusion in the Catechism.
>
> "The Resurrection of Christ is the crowning truth of our faith in Christ" (638). On this score it is necessary to hold two things firmly: the

1. Joseph Cardinal Ratzinger and Christoph Schönborn, *Introduction to the* Catechism of the Catholic Church, trans. Adrian Walker (San Francisco: Ignatius, 1994), 8.

2. Christoph Schönborn, "A Short Introduction to the Four Parts of the Catechism," *Introduction to the* Catechism of the Catholic Church, 64.

Resurrection is both a historical and a transcendent event in one. It is "a real event, with manifestations that were historically verified" (639). The empty tomb is "an essential sign" (640). The appearances of the Risen One and his real, albeit mysterious, corporeity are corroborated by credible historical testimony (641-46). This realism of the salvation event is the basis for its salvific import (651-55).[3]

Does Schönborn Here Envision Approval of Balthasar?

The reference to Balthasar is variously suggested to indicate Schönborn's lack of serious reservations about Balthasar's approach, or his anticipation that Balthasar's theses may (or even will) one day be worthy of inclusion in the Church's catechism; it also might suggest Schönborn's personal judgment of Balthasar's central doctrine. In these views, although Balthasar's ideas "have not yet" achieved the necessary recognition, it is (or is likely) only a matter of time, given how "profound and helpful" they are. Are such interpretations justified by Schönborn's words or by their context?

"However profound and helpful they may be" may indeed suggest that Schönborn agrees with Balthasar. Then again, it may not: Schönborn does not refer exclusively to Balthasar's theology, but speaks generally of "newer interpretations," in the plural. It may be that Schönborn prefers one of the others, although only the most famous (Balthasar's) is identified by name.

Still, the two were friends, so perhaps one ought to infer Schönborn's preference and approval specifically of Balthasar's theology from that relationship. Doing so would be incautious, however, considering how Ratzinger, another friend, admitted he struggled with Balthasar's theses and ultimately could not accept them wholly. Assuming Schönborn's approval or agreement simply on the basis of friendship would also pejoratively suggest Schönborn's criterion for judging theology was personal affection.

Even if the strongest interpretation is taken, that Schönborn himself finds Balthasar's theology of Holy Saturday "profound and helpful" on appropriate principles and himself anticipates an eventual reception for it as common doctrine, it is difficult to see how such a comment could be an

3. Schönborn, "Short Introduction," 74-75.

exercise of his teaching office as a bishop, since no specific affirmation is made about faith or morals. All the comment then would tell us is where he stands as an individual, and his private assessment is not a judgment of the Church as such.

Consider also the opposite situation: even if Schönborn strongly disagreed with Balthasar's theology, one could hardly ask him to write anything other than he did. Should he then have described Balthasar's ideas in negative terms? Recognizing how out of place that would be makes evident how an introduction to the text *as it stands* is not the place for Schönborn to be offering his personal judgments of theological positions that are *not* in the text. If the Church has not yet deemed Balthasar's position acceptable, as Schönborn wrote, why would Schönborn anticipate that decision with his own?

Another thing to consider when reading Schönborn's comment is that, among the "newer interpretations," Balthasar's is certainly the most widespread. It is easy to believe that Schönborn, as a friend of Balthasar and of many who regard Balthasar's theology as indeed "profound and helpful," would often have been asked whether Balthasar's ideas were considered for use in the CCC, and, if not included, why not. What Schönborn wrote actually answers such an implicit question. This interpretation is consistent with the explicit but more general answer he provides when introducing Part Four (Christian Prayer) of the CCC:

> Again and again the criticism has been voiced that the Catechism cites no contemporary theologians. This rests upon a misunderstanding: a catechism does not cite theologians but rather saints, whether they be theologians or "simple believers". The relevance of the Catechism lies not so much in attention to "burning questions" but in the witness of the saints, in whom the faith becomes present and real.[4]

Schönborn's anticipation of an expected question thus is the more credible reason for mentioning Balthasar by name in the context of multiple "newer interpretations" than his taking the opportunity to voice his private opinion. Schönborn's comment leaves open both the possibility of approval and of rejection.

4. Schönborn, "Short Introduction," 95.

What Schönborn Says about the Church's Teaching on Christ's Descent

1) The Descent Is Akin to the Resurrection

Besides overlooking that Schönborn's saying "however profound and helpful [newer interpretations, such as Balthasar's] may be" leaves open precisely the question of exactly how profound and helpful they are, any attempt to invoke Schönborn's comment in support of Balthasar would also have to neglect its immediate and wider contexts. First and significantly, in the "traditional subdivision"[5] of the creed, which the CCC and so Schönborn follow, Christ's descent and His resurrection are regarded as *one article*. This fact alone, that the two are linked together, implies the character of Christ's descent is more akin to His resurrection than to His suffering.

2) The Descent Is Distinct from Christ's Expiatory Death

Moreover, not only are descent and resurrection linked together, the pair is separated and distinguished from Christ's suffering: passion and death are the fourth creedal article, descent and resurrection the fifth.[6] Correspondingly, each article is considered by Schönborn in a unique subsection (d and e). Schönborn also makes the distinction between the two articles explicit when he says the descent–resurrection article "concerns an equally central good of the Christian patrimony of faith" — that is, a truth of the deposit of faith as much at the center of Christianity — as the facts that "Jesus' death is the perfect sacrifice of the new Covenant . . . and . . . an expiatory sacrifice." Christ's death and His descent–resurrection are distinguished, and strongly valued, by being "equally central good[s]."

The distinction Schönborn here acknowledges is significant in two ways for the comparison undertaken in this book. For one, whereas Balthasar tends to treat death as a state of "being dead," the CCC's distinction indicates it is not so. As we saw in the previous chapter, death is the moment that ends earthly life — the soul "separates from the body at death," as the CCC (#366) says — and the descent of the soul follows. (It appears Schönborn inconsistently treats death as a state when, slightly before his commentary on the Christological articles of the creed, he says that "death is the separation of

5. Schönborn, "Short Introduction," 69.
6. Schönborn, "Short Introduction," 72.

body and soul *until the resurrection*."[7] However, since he cites for support CCC ##362-68, which includes the part of #366 just quoted, his expression there, or the translation, inaccurately represents the actual event-language of the CCC.) To be sure, if death is the moment of separation, the continuation of that separation may be called *death* in a secondary sense. The event of separation remains primary, however, as can be seen from the fact that *death* is the noun corresponding to the verb *die*: if death were most properly the state of separation, one would have to say one *is dying* until the resurrection of the body. Instead, we say one *has died* and consequently *is dead*, that is, experiencing the continuing consequence of an action/event completed in the past. Again, if death were the state of being dead, it could not be distinguished from the descent that follows death. Yet the creed and its traditional division of articles distinguishes them, and Schönborn follows suit in his commentary.

The second helpful clarification made by Schönborn based on the traditional division of the creed is that the *death* of Christ on the cross is the perfect expiation, not the descent (as Balthasar would have it): "Jesus' *death* is the *perfect sacrifice* of the new Covenant . . . and . . . an *expiatory sacrifice*." That expiatory sacrifice is brought to perfect completion when Christ said, "'It is finished'; and he bowed his head and gave up his spirit" (Jn 19:30).[8] The last phrase simultaneously signifies the separation of His soul and body (death), and His breathing out of the Spirit at the re-creation of the world in His blood.

3) The Church Has an Identifiable Doctrine of the Descent

The wider context of Schönborn's reference to Balthasar tells us a third important point about the understanding of the descent affirmed in the CCC besides the descent–resurrection link and its separation from the Passion. As Schönborn follows the CCC in distinguishing Christ's death and descent, he explicitly acknowledges that *there is a doctrinal heritage regarding the descent*: the descent–resurrection article is part of "the Christian *patrimony of faith*." Hence the paragraph on Christ's descent "keeps to *what is the common property* of the Church's exegetical tradition." Schönborn here echoes what he says earlier when treating original sin: "It cannot be the task of the Catechism to represent novel theological theses which do not belong to the assured

7. Schönborn, "Short Introduction," 71, emphasis added.

8. See Alyssa Lyra Pitstick, *Light in Darkness: Hans Urs von Balthasar and the Catholic Doctrine of Christ's Descent into Hell* (Grand Rapids: Eerdmans, 2007), 36.

patrimony of the Church's faith."[9] Even Schönborn's mention of "newer interpretations" of the descent (§e) implicitly acknowledges the existence of an older and identifiable understanding of the descent article. After all, it is hardly credible that for nearly two millennia the Church professed Christ's descent without a specific sense of what it was. And indeed, there is ample historical evidence of her belief.[10] It is precisely this faith of the Church about Christ's descent and resurrection — which she *already* possesses — that is "equally central" to what she holds of Christ's death.

Regarding the descent, then, the first duty of Christians must be to seek after what God has revealed about it as transmitted in Scripture and Tradition ("the Church's exegetical tradition"). As Schönborn says when discussing the "I believe" and "We believe" of the creeds,

> *The transmission of divine revelation* takes place by means of the apostolic Tradition, which flows down to us in written and oral Tradition [that is, Scripture and Sacred Tradition, the latter itself conveyed via multiple means] from the one, original source.[11]

Theology is charged to proceed in a manner that illuminates and hands on *that* public revelation. Hence Schönborn quotes John Paul II on fidelity to the Church as one condition of healthy Catholic exegesis: "To be faithful to the Church means to join resolutely the stream of great Tradition."[12] The Church on earth and in heaven is one, and the unity of her faith and Tradition flow from the unity of the Trinity.[13] In consequence,

9. Schönborn, "Short Introduction," 71.

10. Pitstick, *Light in Darkness*, 9-85, provides an introduction to it, including references to more extended treatments of its history. See also Jared Wicks, S.J., "Christ's Saving Descent to the Dead: Early Witnesses from Ignatius of Antioch to Origen," *Pro Ecclesia* 17, no. 3 (Summer, 2008): 281-310.

11. Schönborn, "Short Introduction," 66-67, emphasis in original. My clarification in brackets reflects Schönborn's allusion to *Dei Verbum*, #9.

12. John Paul II, Address on the Occasion of the Celebrations of the First Centenary of the Encyclical *Providentissimus Deus*, the 50th Anniversary of the Encyclical *Divino Afflante Spiritu*, and the Publication of *The Interpretation of the Bible in the Church* (April 23, 1993), #11, quoted in Schönborn, "Major Themes and Underlying Principles of the Catechism of the Catholic Church," *Introduction to the* Catechism of the Catholic Church (San Francisco: Ignatius, 1994), 51.

13. Schönborn, "Major Themes," 40, 50; and "Short Introduction," 78, refers to this original unity of Father, Son, and Holy Spirit and the dependent unities of the Church, her faith, and Tradition (including Scripture).

the consensus of belief of past witnesses to God's revelation (especially the common testimony of the saints[14]) cannot be set aside or contradicted by later generations. Any who do so would, by that very act, separate themselves from the community of faith that goes back to the apostles. The newer speculations on the descent, including specifically Balthasar's, have not yet been judged consistent with the deposit of faith on the descent, which the Church is tasked to preach and hand on. Indeed, they may never be.

4) That Doctrine Affirms Particular Real Events; It Is Not a Mere Metaphor

While Balthasar at best treats the traditional doctrine of the descent as a vague metaphor,[15] in sharp contrast the fourth key thing Schönborn's context tells us is that the Church's faith about Christ's death, descent, and resurrection is no mere metaphor or symbol, but rather an affirmation of realities, the transcendence of which does not diminish their historicity. Indeed, "historical truth itself disappears from sight whenever the dogmatic ground of the Church's faith is abandoned," because "the historical reality of Christian faith is in itself a dogmatic reality," namely, the Son of God taking flesh in time.[16] Although in his commentary on the articles of the creed Schönborn highlights such compatibility of transcendence and historicity specifically in relation to Christ's resurrection, his point applies equally to Passion, death, and descent, for we saw above how he insists it is the "realism of the salvation event" that is "the basis of its salvific import."[17] In other words, Christ's Passion and death can be "redemptive" (§d) and His descent and resurrection "salvific" (§e) only if they are real. A symbol can neither redeem nor save.

Schönborn expands upon this realism in his other contribution to the *Introduction*, "Major Themes and Underlying Principles of the Catechism of the Catholic Church." Dedicating one section to the theme and principle of "Realism in Presenting the Content of Faith," Schönborn says,

14. Schönborn, "Short Introduction," 62, 95.

15. E.g., Hans Urs von Balthasar, *Mysterium Paschale: The Mystery of Easter*, trans. Aidan Nichols (Edinburgh: T. & T. Clark, 1990), 179-80; and *The God Question and Modern Man*, trans. Hilda Graef (New York: Seabury, 1967), 129-30. See also Pitstick, *Light in Darkness*, 329-32. He also erroneously ascribes it only to Eastern Christianity.

16. Schönborn, "Major Themes," 52.

17. Schönborn, "Short Introduction," 75.

> Faith has first of all to do with realities, with facts, not with notions or concepts: '*Fides non terminatur ad enuntiabile sed ad rem* (faith terminates not in propositions but in realities)', said Saint Thomas Aquinas.[18]

Schönborn then highlights how the CCC (#170) itself makes the same point: "We do not believe in formulas, but in those realities they express, which faith allows us to touch," it says, going on to quote the same line from St. Thomas.[19]

5) The Church, including Her Theologians, Is Charged with Handing on That Belief

Schönborn continues with John Paul II's opening words in *Fidei depositum* on the publication of the CCC: "Guarding the deposit of faith is the mission which the Lord entrusted to his Church and which she fulfills in every age." That charge naturally raises a question that Schönborn brings up and answers by quoting John Henry Cardinal Newman:

> What is "the deposit"? [Newman asks]. That which hath been intrusted to you, not which thou hast discovered; what thou hast received, not what thou hast thought out; a matter, not of cleverness, but of teaching; not of private handling, but of public tradition.[20]

Schönborn here effectively answers the question I have consistently raised about Balthasar's theology of Christ's descent into hell: "Is the content of a traditional doctrine binding, or may the verbal formulations be radically reinterpreted?"[21] Put differently, "Is the traditional content (meaning) of the profession of faith as binding as the profession's form (words)?"[22] On Schönborn's principles — via the CCC, St. Thomas, John Paul II, and Newman — the answer is, *The meaning is binding: since our faith concerns realities, not merely words, profession of the words of the creed is meant to be profession of the realities revealed by God.* It is the content of the creed that is the deposit

18. Schönborn, "Major Themes," 55.

19. Schönborn, "Major Themes," 56.

20. Schönborn, "Major Themes," 56, citing "*Essays, Critical and Historical,* I:126," bracketed text supplied by Schönborn.

21. Pitstick, *Light in Darkness,* 342; see also the discussion on 345-46.

22. Alyssa Lyra Pitstick, "Responses to 'Balthasar, Hell, and Heresy,'" *First Things* (March, 2007), 12.

of faith Christ entrusted to His Church, which she has received and teaches in her "public tradition." *Thus the content is as binding as the words; indeed it is even more so, for the words exist for the sake of communicating the content.*

It is conceivable that words might change — even those of the creeds, as their history shows — if the new expressions better convey what originally was meant. Nonetheless, even if the words were to change, the reality communicated must remain the same. As Vatican II says,

> While adhering to the methods and requirements proper to theology, theologians are invited to seek continually for more suitable ways of communicating doctrine to the men of their times. For the deposit of faith or revealed truths are one thing; the manner in which they are formulated without violence to their meaning and significance is another.[23]

* * *

As can be seen, what Schönborn wrote about Balthasar in his *Introduction* neither is an official anticipation by the Church of an eventual embrace of Balthasar's theology of Holy Saturday nor does it necessarily even indicate Schönborn's personal approval. Quite the opposite seems demanded by consistency given what else Schönborn says in the same text about the Church's faith. In particular, the Church's patrimony on Christ's descent affirms His death as His perfect expiation of sin and links His descent with His resurrection. These beliefs contrast with Balthasar's, who extended Christ's passion into His descent, making it the event that completed His atoning sacrifice.

Table 7. *Factors in Schönborn's Introduction that Suggest Balthasar's Theology of Holy Saturday Will Not Be Received by the Church*

The creed and Tradition group Christ's descent with His resurrection.
Those two linked mysteries are together distinguished from Christ's passion and death.
Christ's linked descent and resurrection are of equal importance to His passion and death.

23. Vatican II, Pastoral Constitution on the Church in the Modern World *Gaudium et spes*, #62, in *The Documents of Vatican II*, ed. Walter M. Abbott, S.J., (New York: America Press, 1966), 268.

His death and descent are distinguished from each other.
Christ's death (not His descent) completes His expiatory sacrifice.
The Church's patrimony includes her doctrine on the descent, which already exists and is identifiable.
The Church is charged faithfully to pass on Tradition, which, with Scripture, conveys God's revelation.
The revealed truths to which she thereby witnesses are affirmed as realities, not mere metaphors.

6

THE CRUX OF THE PROBLEM: WHO IS RIGHT?

A dramatic contrast has emerged among the theologies of Christ's descent set forth by Balthasar, Ratzinger/Benedict XVI, and John Paul II. Schönborn's comments about the realism of the Christian profession of faith and the responsibility of the Church to hand it on suggest what is at stake in that difference. Here we come to the crux of the problem, and why, I hazard, many people find criticism of Balthasar unnerving: we have three famous and influential theologians, all currently with conservative reputations, two of them popes, one a saint, one a cardinal, one a cardinal-nominee and winner of the Paul VI prize for his theological contributions — and they disagree on the fundamental meaning of a central article of the faith. They can't all be right. Acknowledging that fact means one must also admit one or more of these widely beloved men is *wrong*. But which one? And what then of Catholic doctrine, if, as rhetorically suggested at the beginning of this book, papal judgment is its standard? Could the situation even provide evidence that the popes are not infallible?

Finding a Standard

Beginning with the question about papal judgment will provide us a standard for answering the question about which theologian is wrong, because, presumably, all three wanted to meet the doctrinal standards of their faith. However, papal judgment, simply speaking, is not the standard for Catholic doctrine. For one thing, "papal judgment" covers too much: the pope teaches authoritatively on matters of faith and morals, not on any topic whatsoever. If the Vatican were to have an office pool for betting on the Super Bowl or World Cup, for example, no one should change bets to match the pope's just because he is the pope.

Even on matters of faith and morals, papal judgment admits to degrees of authority, ranging on a continuum from no more authority than that of private theologians to binding on all Catholics as a matter of faith. Not every statement of a pope is an exercise of his authority, even in theological matters. Benedict XVI's explicit exclusion of his *Jesus of Nazareth* from his pontifical teaching makes that evident: though written by a pope, the book nonetheless carries no papal authority.[1] So authoritative exercise of the office depends not only on topic, but also on intention. (Consequently, as one cannot intend to speak with an authority one does not possess, it should go without saying that papal authority requires actual possession of the office of pope, and does not apply retroactively to the works of a man prior to his election. Consequently, it is unfortunate that, after Ratzinger's election, many of his works have been republished with "Pope Benedict XVI" blazoned on the cover — as though people interested in either Ratzinger or Benedict would fail to know of his election — since this format obscures the new charism given by the reception of papal office and sends conflicting messages about the authority of those texts.)

When it comes to the intentional exercise of actually possessed papal authority related to proper subjects, a distinction is made between what are called the pope's ordinary magisterium (teaching authority) and his extraordinary magisterium. Although the latter is actually more rarely exercised, it is perhaps what people commonly have in mind when they think of papal authority and infallibility. In his extraordinary magisterium, the pope defines a matter of faith and morals that is binding for the entire Church. Because he does so on the basis of the authority Catholics believe Christ uniquely gave to Peter (and so to his successors, the popes), such a judgment is also described as *ex cathedra*, that is, *from the chair*. This expression reflects the fact that historically a sign of authority was to be seated among a standing assembly.

It is Catholic belief that God's grace preserves the pope from error regarding the truths of faith and morality when he teaches *ex cathedra*. God Himself must guarantee that the truth He has revealed is taught through the centuries, because human nature, prone to sin and error, cannot do so. This

1. See also the exposition in Avery Cardinal Dulles, S.J., *Magisterium: Teacher and Guardian of the Faith* (Naples, FL: Sapientia, 2007), 70-81.

preservation by grace when making an *ex cathedra* definition is the infallibility unique to the popes. *Infallibility* comes from the Latin *in*, meaning *not*, and *fallere*, meaning *to deceive*. In other words, in such definitions, a pope will not deceive, will not teach error: he will not teach as false something that is true, nor teach as true something that is false. Definitions taught infallibly in this way are technically called *irreformable*. Infallibility, of course, is to be sharply distinguished from impeccability, which would mean that one does not sin. No one claims that for the popes, least of all the popes themselves!

A case involving *ex cathedra* teaching particularly relevant to our question dates from the 14th century and concerns a disagreement between two popes, John XXII (1316-34) and Benedict XII (1334-42). In 1331, John gave some sermons in which he took the position that the dead do not receive the beatific vision immediately after death, but only after the final judgment and resurrection. Heated debate ensued. After thorough consideration, the matter was permanently settled in 1336 by John's successor, Benedict XII, with the definition in *Benedictus Deus* (quoted in part on the frontispiece and in Chapter 4, and in its entirety in Appendix I).

Benedict XII's *Benedictus Deus* contradicts John XXII's position. Benedict XII makes clear that in every case souls do not have to wait for their recompense until the final resurrection; whether there is any waiting at all depends on their ultimate fate and on when they die: souls that deserve hell have always gone there immediately upon death, while souls that merit heaven have, after any necessary purification (purgatory), only seen God face to face "since the passion and death of the Lord Jesus Christ." In other words, hell has always been open, but heaven was closed until Christ's descent. Avery Cardinal Dulles lists the definition of *Benedictus Deus* first of "the clearest examples" that "most authors would agree" are irreformable.[2] In other words, if *Benedictus Deus*'s definition was not infallibly declared, probably nothing has been.

Indeed, at first glance, such a dispute between two popes seems to provide the one counterexample necessary to prove that the authority of the popes is not infallible. To use the example in this way, however, would merely reveal that one misunderstands what the Church means by that infallibility. What the case really shows is that John's homilies and Benedict's definition are not equally authoritative. As we have already seen, exercise of papal authority requires intention. As the controversy built, John clarified that the question had not yet been settled authoritatively. In effect, he said of his homilies what Benedict XVI has said of his *Jesus of Nazareth*: people were free to agree or

2. Dulles, *Magisterium*, 70.

disagree. So, while John XXII intended in his homilies to articulate his understanding of the faith and even arguments in support of it (in technical terms, to do speculative theology), that is not the same as intending to set forth part of the very deposit of faith in a way binding on all Catholics, which is precisely the intention Benedict XII had in *Benedictus Deus*. It is easiest to see that a papal statement is intended in this authoritative way when marked by formulae such as that used by Benedict XII: "By this Constitution, which is to remain in force forever, we, with apostolic authority, define the following . . ."[3] Benedict XII took care to state explicitly his intention of exercising his full authority. So, John's homilies were not infallible, a fact he also acknowledged by retracting his position before he died,[4] but Benedict's definition is.

It is worth recalling that such definitions do not *make* something to be true, but rather they officially *articulate* and publicly confirm the faith of the Church, simultaneously making clear the Catholic position for those who had doubts or held other ideas. *Benedictus Deus* did not make John XXII to be wrong; he had been wrong all along but now everyone knew clearly. What changes after a dogmatic definition is not the truth, but the degree of certainty with which the truth is known by those who accept the Church's authority.

Of course, the fact that the truth of the faith does not change with such a definition implies that expressions of that faith predate the definition. Something was believed even before the formal definition, which is essentially the difference between doctrine and dogma. The Church holds as true and as identifying for members of her communion many things that have not been dramatically defined as such. For if everyone knows and agrees about something, what need is there to define it? When doctrine (communal belief) is authoritatively defined, typically in response to controversy, it becomes known as dogma. Dogma is thus a subset of doctrine (and consequently, dogmas are sometimes called *doctrine*, taken in its general sense).

It would be a mistake, then, to take papal teaching as true only when expressed in the most formal way of a definition. Doctrine can be true without being dogma. The pope may authoritatively teach Church doctrine and call for the assent of Catholics without proclaiming dogmatic definitions.[5] Whereas in his extraordinary magisterium he can issue *ex cathedra* definitions by his

3. Jacques Dupuis, ed., *The Christian Faith in the Doctrinal Documents of the Catholic Church*, 6th ed. (Staten Island, NY: Alba House, 1996), #2305 (DS 1000).

4. John XXII, *Ne super his* (Dec. 3, 1334), DS 990-91.

5. See, for example, John Paul II, *Ad tuendam fidem* (May 18, 1998), and the corresponding commentary by the Congregation for the Doctrine of the Faith ("Doctrinal Commentary on the Concluding Formula of the *Professio Fidei*," June 29, 1998).

individual authority as pope, when exercising his ordinary magisterium he speaks as head of the college of bishops. (The college is the group of bishops united to the pope, who is himself bishop of Rome. The college itself has an ordinary and extraordinary magisterium, the latter being the definitive teachings of universal councils. Consequently, although we are focusing on the papal magisterium, what is said about authority and infallibility applies also to the bishops' collegial magisterium, except for what is affirmed uniquely of the pope, such as his authority to issue definitions *ex cathedra*, his headship of the college, and the necessity of the other bishops to be united to him.)

But what would make, and indicate, acts of the ordinary papal magisterium as authoritative, if they are not clearly marked the way dogmatic definitions are? This question takes us beyond the rhetorical suggestion that papal judgment is the standard for Catholic doctrine to the real standard, the one that also underpins the authority of the pope, whether exercised in an ordinary or extraordinary (*ex cathedra*) manner.

For even in acts that are intentionally authoritative regarding proper subjects, the pope is accountable by his very office to an external standard. He is called and tasked to internalize that standard to guide his exercise of that office. He is, after all, a deputy; he exercises another's authority. He is judged by that authority even as he serves it with authority: the pope is Vicar of Christ, to whom he is accountable.

Thus a standard exists that measures even papal judgments. That standard is God's Revelation, which Catholics hold is conserved and transmitted in Scripture and Tradition as interpreted by the Magisterium throughout time.[6] (A clarification may be helpful here: in Catholic theology, the word *magisterium* can refer to: 1. a subject, as intended here — the people who exercise teaching authority in the Church, that is, the pope and the bishops in union with him; 2. an object — the body of truths they teach; or 3. a means — the authority by which they teach. When used in the third sense or in adjectival form, the word is not usually capitalized in English.)

There is no circularity in the Magisterium being measured by the Magisterium in this way, because it is current magisterial interpretation that must be consistent with past. As the apostles were commissioned by Christ to preach the truth He revealed, their successors the bishops (including the pope) are tasked by their ordination to teach faithfully that same truth. Conversely, they

6. Vatican II, Dogmatic Constitution on Divine Revelation *Dei Verbum* (Nov. 18, 1965), Ch. II. See also Congregation for the Doctrine of the Faith, "The Primacy of the Successor of Peter in the Mystery of the Church" (October 31, 1998), #7, 10; and Dulles, *Magisterium*, 71-72.

have no authority to preach what they have not received. Any preaching of something that is not Christ's truth does not carry authority. Since the community of faith is identified by its faith, if the community is to remain one, the same faith must endure as well. (It follows that the "development" of any particular belief is the unfolding of the significance *of that belief*, not the changing of it into its opposite or something else incompatible; in this way, the faith both retains its identity and is living.[7] It also follows that one separates from that community by dissent from her identifying profession of faith.)

Besides the need for consistency in magisterial interpretation across time, since that interpretation is in service of Scripture and Tradition, those vessels of divine revelation provide an objective measure on a still deeper level. Most foundationally of all, because it is Christ who commissioned the college of apostles (and in them, their successors) as the organ for authoritatively teaching His truth, He Himself, the Word of God, is the ultimate source and standard of the authority of Church teaching.

That means that He also preserves the exercise of their charge from error. Just like what was said of the pope's *ex cathedra* definitions above, God must guarantee His truth is taught when the successors of the apostles teach the faith received from the apostles, because it is precisely for the teaching of that truth throughout time that Christ established the apostolic office of the Twelve and frail human nature could not sustain that charge unaided across the centuries. In other words, God's gift of infallibility must apply not only to dogma, but also to doctrine, where *doctrine* does not mean just anything that is taught, by just any theologian or priest or even individual bishop, but rather it signifies the deposit of faith, the corporate belief of the Church, in continuity with the apostles.

In short, when the ordinary Magisterium is *both* ordinary *and* universal, it is infallible.[8] It must be, because the charism of infallibility exists precisely

7. For those who would like to consider more what such continuity within development entails, Blessed John Henry Newman discusses some distinguishing characteristics of authentic development in his famed *Essay on the Development of Christian Doctrine*. As for whether Balthasar's theology of Holy Saturday possesses those characteristics, I consider that question in my article, "Development of Doctrine, or Denial? Balthasar's Holy Saturday and Newman's *Essay*," *International Journal of Systematic Theology* 11, no. 2 (April 2009): 129-45.

8. Dulles, *Magisterium*, 70, says the pope's ordinary Magisterium is not infallible; Ludwig Ott, *Fundamentals of Catholic Dogma* (Rockford, IL: Tan, 1974), 10, says the same. Ott refers to Vatican I as evidence, but the relevant passage (DS 3073-74) only affirms the infallibility of the pope's *ex cathedra* teaching, without pronouncing on his ordinary Magisterium.

In contrast, Dulles (*Magisterium*, 88, emphasis added) says that the truths taught by the "ordinary *and universal* Magisterium" are to be held with "firm faith" (Profession of Faith) or "divine and Catholic faith" (Vatican I; see DS 3011), because they are part of divine revelation

for the purpose of passing on with certainty the truth received from Christ by the apostles, and most of what the Church believes has not been dogmatically defined by acts of extraordinary magisterium. Rather, it has been consistently taught and accepted *as the faith of the Church*, as the belief of the community whose identity stretches back to the apostles and to Christ. What then indicates the acts of the ordinary papal magisterium as authoritative and potentially infallible is their consistency with God's Revelation, transmitted in Scripture and Tradition as interpreted by the Magisterium through time.

So in our example, John XXII's homilies were certainly an exercise of his ordinary magisterium, his day-to-day attempt to live out his episcopal commission. However, the resulting controversy essentially concerned whether they were taught according to the ordinary *and universal* magisterium, that is, whether his ideas represented the faith of the Church as such. Benedict XII's *ex cathedra* definition expressed an infallible judgment that they were not and did not.

Of course, some non-Catholics will not agree the pope and bishops have the authority here described; as they wish, they may pursue in other texts the Catholic arguments on its behalf. (Frank Sheed's classic, *Theology and Sanity*, is always a good place to begin, as is Karl Keating's *Catholicism and Fundamentalism*, which is particularly attentive to Scripture and to Protestant concerns.[9])

(cf. CCC #892). As the charism of infallibility exists precisely for the authoritative teaching of the truths of revelation (Dulles, *Magisterium*, 59-66), it follows this ordinary *and universal* Magisterium must be infallible.

Donald W. Wuerl, *The Catholic Way: Faith for Living Today* (New York: Doubleday, 2011), 108, like Dulles, but more explicitly, draws attention to such a distinction between the "ordinary magisterium" and the "ordinary and universal magisterium." He is also emphatic that the latter is infallible (108-9).

In instances of the ordinary and universal magisterium, the certainty of the teaching would come not from the pope's *individual* authority, as it would for *ex cathedra* proclamations, but from the authority of the college of bishops (including the pope) as the successors to the apostles, that is, from the authority of the Magisterium universal in space and time. To be clear, I am not here saying that the pope receives his authority from the college, but rather that the college, including the pope, receives their authority in virtue of being successors to the apostles, and this presumes a unity of belief between contemporary bishops and their predecessors. This understanding of the reliability of ordinary and universal teaching seems reasonable given the analogous situation in the Congregation for the Doctrine of the Faith, Commentary on the *Professio*, #9, which is explicit that the ordinary and universal Magisterium is infallible.

9. Both are published by Ignatius Press. In the 1993 edition of Sheed, one might consult particularly pages 279-310, while in the 1998 edition of Keating, see pages 198-231.

We have now identified a standard our three Catholic theologians would themselves agree should measure their work: God's Revelation, transmitted in Scripture and Tradition as interpreted by the Magisterium. One place that authoritative standard is articulated is in the universal catechisms, as John Paul II makes clear in *Fidei depositum* (*Guarding the Deposit of Faith*):

> [A] catechism should faithfully and systematically present the teaching of Sacred Scripture, the living Tradition in the Church and the authentic Magisterium . . . to allow for a better knowledge of the Christian mystery and for enlivening the faith of the People of God.[10]

In the same document, John Paul II says the *Catechism of the Catholic Church* (CCC) meets this standard.[11] While it is conceivable that local catechisms may meet that standard more or less effectively,[12] the *Roman Catechism* (RC) surely fulfills it, since like the CCC, it was promulgated for the entire Church and its goal was to aid believers in being unified in faith. The bishops of the Council of Trent

> deemed it of the first importance that a work should appear, sanctioned by the authority of the Council, from which pastors and all others on whom the duty of imparting instruction devolves, may be able to seek and find reliable matter for the edification of the faithful; that, as there is "one Lord, one faith" (Eph 4:5) there may also be one standard and prescribed form of propounding the dogmas of faith.[13]

This work is the RC, which is consequently also known as the *Catechism of the Council of Trent*.

Indeed, since the RC's promulgation by Pope St. Pius V, the popes have

10. John Paul II, *Fidei depositum*, #2, translated and reproduced in CCC.

11. John Paul II, *Fidei depositum*, #3.

12. Consider, for example, *The Church's Confession of Faith: A Catholic Catechism for Adults*, trans. Stephen Wentworth Arndt, ed. Mark Jordan (San Francisco: Ignatius, 1987). Walter Kasper was its primary author, and readers of this book will be able to discern whether his principal source for his presentation of Christ's descent into hell was Balthasar, Ratzinger, or the Church's doctrine as expressed in the RC (it being the only universal catechism published at that time).

13. *Catechism of the Council of Trent*, 4. The format of the internal quotation has been changed to follow contemporary convention: the text, originally italicized, has been placed in quotes and the citation, originally footnoted, has been placed in parentheses.

repeatedly commended it as a reliable exposition of the Catholic faith. For example, Clement XIII said that, in it is "compiled the teaching which is common to the whole Church and which is far removed from every danger of error."[14] "For the abundance and accuracy of its teaching," Leo XII described it as "a precious summary of the whole of theology, dogmatic and moral."[15] John Paul II himself called it "a work of the first rank as a summary of Christian teaching and traditional theology."[16]

These commendations, like that of the CCC, do not mean the texts are written in irreformable statements, but that the doctrine taught is a reliable expression of Catholic belief and is, as far as Catholic belief is concerned, true. So, while *how* a belief was *expressed* might be tweaked, what the Catholic Church would hold as certainly true is the reality that expression is meant to communicate.[17]

The Fathers of the Council of Trent did not intend the RC to articulate the Church's faith accurately only for those alive at the time. On the contrary, their explicit purpose was to unify Catholics in their faith by establishing norms for instruction, which of its nature shapes the future. If what they said about Christ's descent was true then, it is still true. Consequently, the RC and CCC should always be read together, for if one has authority because it is a universal catechism, so does the other. Due to the RC's historical context, it feels the need to be very explicit, so it helps clarify the truths the CCC expresses in the more oblique language of our own time.

Application of the Standard

We now have identified a standard for answering the major question of this chapter. For if we take the RC and the CCC as important authoritative statements of Catholic belief (as they are intended to be and are), ones that help articulate the standard by which even papal teaching is measured, they can aid us to discern which of our three theologians present a Catholic doctrine of Christ's descent and so are right, at least from the perspective of Catholic belief. Any concerns about circularity in judging John Paul II by the CCC, which he promulgated, can be put to rest by using also the RC, which predates all three men.

14. Clement XIII, Encyclical *In Dominico Agro* (On Instruction in the Faith) (June 14, 1761), #4.

15. Leo XIII, *Dépuis le jour* (September 8, 1899), #23.

16. John Paul II, Apostolic Exhortation *Catechesi Tradendae* (October 16, 1979), #13.

17. See CCC, #170: "We do not believe in formulae, but in those realities they express."

As we saw in Chapter 4, John Paul II's theology of the descent is completely consistent with both universal catechisms. While *Benedictus Deus* was identifiable as authoritative amid controversy due to its form as a dogmatic definition, John Paul II's audience on the descent is identifiable as authoritative from its consistency with past Church teaching.[18]

Although comparison of Ratzinger and Benedict XVI with that standard is complicated by his ambiguity, hesitation, and metaphorical use of "descent into hell," it appears he does not contradict it in substance and even obliquely affirms it. Benedict XVI most recently presented the descent entirely (although indirectly) along traditional lines while his earlier language of image might also have been meant to describe the historical event itself. Ratzinger's idea of Christ's pre-death psychological anguish coupled with a transformation of the afterlife through His presence as communion is compatible in general terms with both catechisms if his references to the descent are read in their fuller contexts, as presented here in Chapters 2 and 3.

Balthasar's theses, on the other hand, conflict with the doctrine of the two catechisms, and this difference is not simply a matter of appearance or expression: Balthasar denies some fundamental beliefs the catechisms affirm, including where Christ descended and what He did there.

A Supporting Consideration: Possession of Teaching Authority

While consistency (or not) with the catechisms is decisive, another consideration provides additional support for this conclusion: John Paul II and Benedict, Ratzinger and Balthasar, do not have equal teaching authority. As popes, John Paul II and Benedict have equal authority, of course. Since Benedict does not engage what happened in the descent directly, by default John Paul II's exposition in that regard must be given weight. John Paul II intentionally and explicitly expounds the truth of the historic event and its significance. Benedict initially focuses just on the latter. Benedict's early approach admits compatibility with his predecessor, while in his later television interview, he obliquely concurs with John Paul II also on the event itself. Significantly, despite Ratzinger's friendship with Balthasar and his attraction

18. Besides the universal catechisms, on the consistency of that teaching, see, e.g., Alyssa Lyra Pitstick, *Light in Darkness: Hans Urs von Balthasar and the Catholic Doctrine of Christ's Descent into Hell* (Grand Rapids: Eerdmans, 2007), 9-85.

to some elements of his thought, as Pope Benedict XVI he has not taken up or affirmed any of Balthasar's theses. Instead, he has increasingly explicitly aligned himself with John Paul II and other official expressions of Catholic belief about Christ's descent. Despite differences in vocabulary, style, and tone, there is no real opposition between the popes.

The degree of teaching authority exercised in their particular statements should also be considered. Since Benedict himself explicitly stated his *Jesus of Nazareth* is his work as a private theologian, it carries no magisterial authority. As he himself said, each person is free to agree or disagree with it. Of course, the text may carry a kind of personal authority for individual readers to the extent each one considers Ratzinger's theology generally a reliable guide to the faith. One reader may regard it highly, another may not, still another may value only particular parts. Of course, since theology aims to help us understand the reality we believe, fidelity to that faith and to reason measures whether someone ought personally to take a particular theologian as an authority or not.

As for the magisterial texts of Benedict and John Paul II, other things being equal, audiences generally are considered to be less authoritative than, say, encyclicals (and encyclicals less than apostolic constitutions, such as *Benedictus Deus*). In this light, Benedict XVI's encyclical, *Spe salvi*, would be more authoritative than John Paul II's 1989 audience.

Of course, the vehicle of teaching is not the only thing to consider. The manifest purpose of the documents is also relevant. *Spe salvi* is an encyclical on Christian hope, not on Christ's descent into hell; indeed, the descent appears only briefly, metaphorically, and tangentially there. John Paul II's 1989 audience, on the other hand, explicitly focuses on Christ's descent. In it, John Paul II aims precisely at setting forth the Catholic understanding on this article of faith since the audience is part of his catechesis on the creed. He also repeatedly stresses certain elements consistent with Scripture, Sacred Tradition, and earlier magisterial teaching on Christ's descent, including the definitive *Benedictus Deus*. This evidence of his intention, sources, and continuity support the conclusion that the audience is an exercise of his ordinary and universal teaching authority, at least in regard to those points he emphasized, namely, that Christ's own beatitude is shared with the holy dead in His descent after the separation of His body and soul by death. The audience then is more authoritative in regard to Christ's descent than *Spe salvi*, which only mentions the descent in passing and metaphorically.

As for Ratzinger's teaching authority, his *Introduction to Christianity*, *Eschatology*, and "Meditations" were written before his ordination as bishop in

1977, and so are indisputably private works. Although his 1997 introduction to the "Meditations" comes after that ordination, it appears simply to be an introduction to his earlier reflections rather than an instance of intentional episcopal teaching. Such an exercise of office in any case would presume appropriate union of faith and practice with the college of bishops, including its head, the pope.[19] In 1997, John Paul II was pope, of course, and he had already explicitly reaffirmed the traditional doctrine of the descent in detail. Moreover, for any exercise of episcopal teaching office, including Ratzinger's, authentically to be such, it must be consistent with the faith handed on from the apostles, for the transmission of that faith is the very purpose for which the office exists. Union with the college of bishops (meaning necessarily at minimum, its head, the pope) contemporary to any bishop is sign and instrument of this unity that transcends time.

Finally, Balthasar has no magisterial teaching authority. As for whether his readers ought to take him as a personal authority, that depends at least on the two criteria mentioned earlier, fidelity to the faith and to reason. Suggestive in this regard is the incompatibility of his theses on the descent with the doctrine as explicitly presented in the RC. (The CCC was published only after his death.) Other evidence related to those criteria is discussed in my previous book, *Light in Darkness: Hans Urs von Balthasar and the Catholic Doctrine of Christ's Descent into Hell.*[20]

* * *

We need to be upfront and acknowledge exactly what it is that Balthasar's theology contradicts: in *Fidei depositum,* John Paul II explained that the Church's catechisms aim to "faithfully and systematically present the teaching of Sacred Scripture, the living Tradition in the Church and the authentic Magisterium." So, despite Balthasar's extensive use of Scripture, despite the claims to a development in doctrine made by his followers, despite his intention to serve the Magisterium and his defense of the papacy, to the extent that his theology of Holy Saturday contradicts one or both of the universal catechisms, it does not represent "the teaching of Sacred Scripture, the living Tradition in the Church and the authentic Magisterium."

19. Dulles, *Magisterium,* 49, see also pages 57-58.

20. On problems in Balthasar's coherence and self-consistency, see, e.g., Pitstick, *Light in Darkness,* 94 fn. 30, 111, 126, 128-29, 160-63, 261-62, 271-73, 289, 308-10, 312, 323, and 326. As for matters of doctrine, *Light in Darkness* particularly examines issues relating to Christ, see, e.g., 281-302.

7

THE CRUX, CONTINUED: JOHN PAUL II'S AND RATZINGER/BENEDICT XVI'S PRAISE OF BALTHASAR

The conclusions of the previous chapter only sharpen the difficulty of the other question we raised in the introduction, however. Let us grant that John Paul II's position is authoritative, that Benedict XVI may reasonably be understood to be consistent with his predecessor, and that Balthasar's view of Christ's descent is not right, at least as measured by the Catholic standard of the universal catechisms. What about the fact that John Paul II and Benedict have praised Balthasar precisely for his theological contributions? One side of our dilemma was the disagreement among the three on what happened in Christ's descent, the other is the admiration these two had generally for Balthasar and his work.

Possible Approaches to a Resolution

One resolution would be to deny any substantive theological differences in their theologies of the descent. From the evidence we have seen, such a position is untenable unless one is ignorant of their individual conclusions or deliberately blind to their differences.

Another approach would be to deny papal infallibility: If the popes praised a man for his theology and that theology is wrong, are the popes then not infallible? A brute affirmation of papal infallibility in the face of this question results in self-contradiction: for if the statements of praise are infallibly true and specifically refer to Balthasar's theology of Holy Saturday, then the popes' own teaching on the descent was wrong —

which means the popes are not infallible — but then neither is their praise of Balthasar.

In fact, the challenge to papal infallibility actually shows that the way forward follows our earlier observation that not all papal judgments are authoritative: the popes still possess the charism of infallibility even if not all situations involve an exercise of it. So the real question is, What force of authority does this praise have?

Cardinal Ratzinger's Eulogy of Balthasar

To make a judgment, we need to look at the evidence. What exactly has been said? Perhaps the most well-known instance occurred at Balthasar's funeral, when Cardinal Ratzinger highlighted the Johannine, Ignatian, and Marian characteristics of Balthasar's life. He also commented that although Balthasar did not live to receive the cardinal's hat,

> What the Pope intended to express by this mark of distinction [*Geste der Anerkennung*, so more accurately: gesture of acknowledgement, recognition, or appreciation], and of honor, remains valid: no longer only private individuals but the Church itself, in its official responsibility, tells us that he is right in what he teaches of the faith [*er ein rechter Lehrer des Glaubens ist*: he is a right/real/genuine teacher of the faith], that he points the way [he is *ein Wegweiser*: one who knows the way] to the sources of living water — a witness to the Word which teaches us Christ and which teaches us how to live.[1]

Although eulogies as a genre are known for exaggeration, Ratzinger's comments should not be dismissed so quickly. The statement is extraordinary: "The Church itself, in its official responsibility, tells us that [Balthasar] is right in what he teaches of the faith, that he points the way to the sources of living water." The latter phrase is unproblematic in our context for it does not touch on Balthasar's specific conclusions about Holy Saturday. Scripture and the Fathers are certainly "sources of living water" to which Balthasar

1. Joseph Ratzinger, "Homily at the Funeral Liturgy for Hans Urs von Balthasar," *Communio ICR* 15 (Winter, 1988): 515, translation supplemented from original, "Homilie beim Gedenkgottesdienst für Hans Urs von Balthasar," *Internationale katholische Zeitschrift Communio*, 17, no. 1 (January, 1988): 476.

points; in this, he is "a witness to the Word which teaches us Christ and which teaches us how to live."

So what attracts attention is the phrase, "The Church itself, in its official responsibility, tells us that he is right in what he teaches of the faith." What does this phrase mean? Certainly Ratzinger means at least so much: that "the Church in its official responsibility," that is, in the person of John Paul II, her earthly head and representative, desired and intended to give him the honor of the cardinalate in recognition of his theology.

Is the use of "official responsibility" meant to indicate that what follows ("he is right," etc.) was made by an infallible pronouncement? Such a conclusion would be warranted neither by the person speaking (Ratzinger, who was not pope), nor by the form of address (no quotation of a formal exercise of office by John Paul II). It is also doubtful whether the subject (whether Balthasar is a sound teacher) is appropriate matter for an exercise of infallibility, since typically such exercise directly concerns God's revelation regarding faith or morals.

What, more precisely, about Balthasar's theology is deserving of recognition? "He is right in what he teaches of the faith"; we can translate the original more accurately, "He is a right [or 'real,' 'genuine'] teacher of the faith." If one understood this to mean he is *right in everything* he says about the Catholic faith, it would be extraordinary approval, indeed. It is impossible, however, that John Paul II intended to say Balthasar was infallible in this way, since the pope himself is not infallible in everything he says, even in matters of faith and morals: as we saw, infallibility requires not merely appropriate topics, but also intentional exercise of the magisterial office by one who holds it.

If we cannot go so far as to extend to Balthasar an infallibility greater than the pope's, what then does the statement mean? "He is right in what he teaches of the faith" could mean that to the extent he teaches the (true) faith, he is right in it. This is something of a non-statement, a tautology. Given Ratzinger's personal approbation of much, but not all, of Balthasar, we may assume he hoped to say more in the eulogy of a beloved friend. Still, this modest signification is affirmed by the phrase "being a right teacher of the Faith" being in apposition with "that he points [or knows] the way to the sources of living water," to the Word that teaches us Christ and how to live. He rightly teaches the faith (or is a "genuine teacher") in that he knows (or "points") the way to that Word. So much is safe, both for the listeners to understand and the speaker to claim. More than that results in Balthasar having a charism of truth broader than the popes'. Given Ratzinger's own status as a theologian, one may reasonably assume he had a sufficiently nuanced sense of infallibility to avoid having intended any such thing.

Pope John Paul II's Note of Condolence

The value of the funeral homily for claiming papal approval of Balthasar rests on Ratzinger's underlying reference to John Paul II. What did John Paul II himself say, however, that forms the basis for Ratzinger's paraphrase? Ratzinger may have in mind the note of personal commemoration John Paul II sent him before the funeral:

> All who knew the priest, von Balthasar, are shocked, and grieve over the loss of a great son of the Church, an outstanding man of theology and of the arts, who deserves a special place of honor in contemporary ecclesiastical and cultural life.
>
> *It was my wish to acknowledge and to honor in a solemn fashion the merits [Balthasar] earned through his long and tireless labors as a spiritual teacher and as an esteemed scholar by naming him to the dignity of the Cardinalate* in the last Consistory. . . .
>
> Your participation at the solemn funeral services . . . will be an expression of the high esteem in which the person and the life-work of this great priest and theologian are held by the Holy See. . . . Now that his earthly life is completed, may *he, who was for many a spiritual leader on the way to faith*, be granted the vision of God, face to face.[2]

Here are the same motifs of official acknowledgement and honor of a spiritual teacher on the way of faith as are found in Ratzinger's homily.

The intended form of recognition was for Balthasar to be raised to the cardinalate. Since he died unexpectedly before that could happen (hence John Paul II refers to him as a priest), John Paul II substitutes, as it were, an official mandate for Ratzinger to participate in the funeral. Yet this commendation by no means amounts to papal approval of specific theses of Balthasar nor even of his theology as a whole. It merely recognizes indisputable facts: besides being a man of uncommon culture, Balthasar spent his long life leading many in their spiritual life and contributing to theological scholarship in a way that distinguished him, even to the pope.

2. John Paul II, "Telegram," *Communio*, 15, no. 4 (1988): 511, emphasis added.

If John Paul II's note is the basis for Ratzinger's funeral comment, to take Ratzinger's words as saying anything more would be to go beyond John Paul II's stated intention.

Pope Benedict XVI's Message on Balthasar's Centenary

The next instance of praise to examine occurred after Ratzinger's election as Benedict XVI. In 2005, Benedict gave a message to the participants of a conference celebrating the centenary of Balthasar's birth. If John Paul II's intention of making Balthasar a cardinal or Ratzinger's characterization of it had been meant as a sort of *ex cathedra* or *carte blanche* approval, Benedict should have had no hesitation to reiterate it. As pope himself, however, he was more circumspect than he was as cardinal in characterizing Balthasar's authority.

In his message, Benedict highlights Balthasar's focus on the Incarnation in his theology, the fact that he placed his work at the service of the Church, and that he knew the importance of continual conversion through prayer. Benedict elaborates this last characteristic as the example "of a true theologian who in contemplation had discovered a consistent course of action for giving Christian witness in the world."[3] About his theology generally, Benedict says,

> I am convinced that his theological reflections preserve their freshness and profound relevance undiminished to this day and that they incite many others to penetrate ever further into the depths of the mystery of the faith, [held by the hand by such an authoritative guide].[4]

While Balthasar's objective popularity would seem to confirm Benedict's comments about the freshness, relevance, and motivational power of his works, the statement just quoted expresses personal valuation and assessment, not official teaching. There is no use of the formulae belonging

3. Benedict XVI, "Message to the Participants in the International Convention on the Occasion of the Centenary of the Birth of the Swiss Theologian Hans Urs von Balthasar" (October 6, 2005).

4. Benedict XVI, "Message." Brackets indicate a correction to the translation, which added "leading them" in "with such an authoritative guide leading them by the hand." The original is simply "*tenuti per mano da una guida così autorevole*" (Benedict XVI, Messagio [October 6, 2005]).

to definitive statements nor is it a reiteration of teachings of the ordinary Magisterium.

Even if one wanted to read it as taking a stronger position, what precisely would it be affirming? The freshness and relevance of Balthasar's reflections, and the motivation they provide many. Such a broad generalization invites questions: Are all his reflections relevant? Are they equally relevant? In what way are they relevant? And so on. In short, those who would interpret this praise strongly would be hard pressed to unfold its meaning in a substantive way in support of any specific thesis of Balthasar. Benedict affirms nothing here in detail.

"With such an authoritative guide" to hold their hand: questions similar to those just raised likewise have to be asked here. Balthasar's authority apparently comes from his knowledge of "the mystery of the faith," since he is to be a guide to others into its depths. Does this authority characterize all his reflections? Equally? Although Benedict's comment reveals that he personally considers Balthasar an authoritative guide, that is not the case in everything. As he had explicitly stated only six years earlier, he did not agree with Balthasar on the descent; he did not think he was right.

Ratzinger's eulogy and Benedict's message make his love and admiration for Balthasar unmistakable, but neither form nor content of what he has said amounts to blanket approval of all Balthasar wrote, much less specific approval of Balthasar's theology of Holy Saturday. Those who use his words to suggest otherwise — some websites seem rather overenthusiastic in this regard — irresponsibly misrepresent them.

Pope John Paul II's "Favorite Theologian"?

In looking at Ratzinger's interpretation of John Paul II's intention to make Balthasar a cardinal, we have already seen something of John Paul II's view of Balthasar in John Paul II's own words. What other evidence is there with which to flesh out the Polish pontiff's perspective still more fully?

I not infrequently hear that Balthasar was John Paul II's "favorite theologian." Who says this? More to the point, where does John Paul II say it? Every place I have seen the statement, it is made without citation. My attempts to locate the original or an equivalent have proven unfruitful. (If any reader can document its source in John Paul II, I would be grateful.) It appears to be a case of websites recirculating each other's content.

Nonetheless, even if it cannot be verified, let us suppose this claim to be true. Balthasar was John Paul II's favorite theologian; what does that tell us? Certainly it indicates admiration and appreciation; it might also indicate a certain inspiration and appropriation, though it would be imprudent to speculate about the degree or specific content of that influence on the basis of such a general comment. To assume a universal influence upon John Paul II would reduce his thought to an intellectual slavishness inconsistent with the originality found in his works; besides, it simply would not hold up to a comparison of the two men's works. If it is not warranted to presume so great a degree of influence, we again return to John Paul II allowing for the possibility of error in Balthasar. Indeed, the fact that the teaching on Christ's descent in John Paul II's catechesis on the descent and in the catechism he promulgated, as well as in his audiences of October 19 and 26, 1988, contradict so many of the central theses unique to Balthasar's *descensus* theology imply that he did consider, or would have considered, Balthasar in actual error on those points.

Pope John Paul II's Conferral of the Paul VI Prize on Balthasar

Balthasar's devotees often highlight, however, that in 1984, just four years before Balthasar's death, John Paul II conferred on him the Paul VI Prize for his theological contributions. So, again, let us look at the evidence, the prize and John Paul II's involvement with it.

At the prize ceremony itself, the president of the Paul VI Institute, Giuseppe Camadini, explained the motivation for awarding Balthasar the prize, saying,

> The Scientific and Executive Commitees of the Institute of Paul VI of Brescia, in the joint session of Feb. 4, 1984, convened according to the Statute and Rule, deliberated with unanimous vote to confer the 1984 International Paul VI Prize to the most reverend and illustrious professor Hans Urs von Balthasar of Basel, for his considerable contribution ["]to the development of religious inquiry and knowledge["[5]] in the area of theological studies, with the following motivation: . . .[6]

5. Quotation marks are inserted to indicate material drawn from the rules governing the prize (*Regolamento del Premio*, a. 1, as cited in John Paul II's address at the ceremony).

6. "La Motivazione del Premio," *Hans Urs von Balthasar: Premio Internazionale Paolo VI, 1984* (Brescia: Istituto Paolo VI, 1984), 25.

Camadini goes on to identify three motivating elements: Balthasar's "vast and profound culture," "the many facets and the breadth of his work," and the "originality and boldness of his conceptions."[7] In elaborating them, Camadini maintains that Balthasar's thought "has been appreciated for its intrinsic value" and is "destined to become a 'classic' in the theological tradition and especially in the new Catholic systematics."[8] He also mentions how, alone among his contemporaries in having attempted a *summa*, Balthasar's work was enriched by an extraordinary grasp of human culture.[9] The quality of his writing and commitment to theology as rooted in Christian existence made him "an author of great influence, also with respect to 'spiritual' formation in the highest and most complete sense of the word."[10] Again, high praise; again — except for the prediction, which by its genre, is open to debate — indisputable.

In the context of our question of John Paul II's regard for Balthasar, what is noteworthy about Camadini's presentation? First, the decision to confer the prize on Balthasar was made by the Scientific and Executive Committees of the Paul VI Institute — and John Paul II was not on the rosters of members. In other words, John Paul II did not choose the recipient of the prize, and officially he had nothing to do with the selection as he was not a member of either committee. Did he nominate or propose Balthasar? Perhaps. Of course, that is speculation. Given what Camadini said about Balthasar, it is likely the members were themselves sufficiently acquainted and impressed with Balthasar to have generated the nomination. But for the sake of the argument, let us assume John Paul II was the source of the nomination.

Second, John Paul II agreed to present the prize and himself gave an address at the prize ceremony. Was this simply an official function to be fulfilled as part of his position? Although biographies of John Paul II and Balthasar do not particularly highlight their relationship, I assume quite the opposite, especially given what we saw John Paul II will say in his note to Ratzinger for Balthasar's funeral. Let us assume that instead of merely going along with the Committees' decision, John Paul II approved it wholeheartedly and even was the one who nominated Balthasar. What did he have to say on this opportunity to recognize and praise Balthasar, potentially his "favorite theologian"?

7. "Motivazione," 25.
8. "Motivazione," 25.
9. "Motivazione," 25.
10. "Motivazione," 25-26.

After his greeting, John Paul II begins by mentioning his personal affection for Paul VI, for whom the Institute and the Prize are named. He then goes on to express his appreciation of the Institute itself and to recall that persons or institutions receive the prize for having "contributed in a considerable way to the development of religious inquiry and knowledge,"[11] a phrase drawn from the rules governing the prize. He then says,

> I extend my warm congratulations to Prof. Hans Urs von Balthasar. May the declaration of esteem, given to him with the award of this prize, comfort him for his completed labor and help him to continue the research in which he has already attained such significant results. The passion for theology that sustained his task of reflection upon the works of the Fathers, the theologians, and the mystics receives today an important recognition. He placed his vast knowledge at the service of an "understanding of the faith," which was able to show to contemporary man the splendor of truth that emanates from Jesus Christ. Today's ceremony intends to acknowledge that and express such recognition.[12]

John Paul II then commends the Institute for having selected theology as the area for its very first prize since it is the science that especially contributes to the "development of religious inquiry and knowledge."[13] This comment provides the transition to the main body of John Paul II's address, in which he reflects on theology as service to truth, to revealed truth, to the Church, and to the Magisterium. Beginning to close his address, John Paul II calls to mind the "spiritual closeness"[14] of Paul VI by reading a few sentences his predecessor had quoted from Balthasar on the absolute centrality of the Word, of Christ.[15] Having encouraged theologians in general and before ending with his blessing, he says,

11. *Regolamento del Premio*, a. 1, cited in John Paul II, "Il Discorso del Santo Padre Giovanni Paolo II," in *Balthasar: Premio*, 9. This speech is titled "Discorso di Giovanni Paolo II in Occasione della Consegna del 'Premio Internazionale Paolo VI' ad Hans Urs von Balthasar" on the Vatican website.

12. John Paul II, "Discorso," 10.

13. *Regolamento del Premio*, a. 1, cited in John Paul II, "Discorso," 10.

14. John Paul II, "Discorso," 13.

15. John Paul II's reference is to "Esort. Ap. 'Quinque iam anni', *Insegnamenti*, VIII, 1970, 1422."

> I renew my congratulations [or satisfaction, pleasure] and my wishes to Professor Urs von Balthasar, who has dedicated his whole life to theological inquiry as loving contemplation of God and service to the Church.[16]

In this address, John Paul II chooses to spend most of his time on the service of theology generally. He encourages Balthasar to continue his research, which has proven fruitful, and commends him specifically for his service and dedication. No one can dispute Balthasar saw himself, and set himself, at the service of the Church. But such generous dedication, even sustained over a lifetime, does not in itself guarantee perfectly reliable results. John Paul II did not commend Balthasar for this or that particular result or insight. Nor, for that matter, did the selection Committees. All highlighted general traits, but such are insufficient to conclude approbation of any particular thesis, such as Balthasar's doctrine of the descent.

* * *

To the best of my knowledge, these are all the papal statements published in relation to Balthasar's theology as such. There is certainly praise of the man and praise of the theologian, but there is no approbation of specific theses, least of all his theology of Holy Saturday, with which Ratzinger explicitly said he could not concur and with which John Paul II took an incompatible position in his papal audiences and promulgation of the CCC. We have then a clear distinction between the person and at least one of his positions, though significantly it is the one at the heart of Balthasar's theology. One might admire the man in many respects without approving of all his specific theological theses.

Even if one were to interpret Ratzinger's, Benedict's, and John Paul II's statements of admiration more strongly than their words justify, as Edward T. Oakes does in his partial exposition of the popes' comments on Balthasar mentioned at the beginning of this book,[17] not every utterance of a pope is infallible and what is said of Balthasar does not bear the necessary marks for infallibility.

16. John Paul II, "Discorso," 13.

17. For example, Edward T. Oakes, S.J., "*Descensus* and Development: A Response to Recent Rejoinders," *International Journal of Systematic Theology*, 13, no. 1 (January, 2011): 14 n. 26, and 17 n. 32.

CONCLUSION

Before World War II, the traditional doctrine of Christ's triumphal descent to the souls of the just was, as one historian put it, so well known as *the* Catholic doctrine that there was no debate about it.[1] Indeed, many of the Protestant reformers distinguished themselves deliberately from the Catholic Church by explicitly rejecting the "papist" doctrine of that glorious descent to the limbo of the Fathers. They proposed instead, for example, some experience of the horrors and anguish of the hell of eternal punishment either before or after death.

Since faith concerns realities, the Church believes the articles of the creed not as mere sounds or independent words strung together, but as whole propositions intended to communicate specific meaning about reality.[2] The content of the creed is the deposit of faith that Christ entrusted to His Church. As the articles of the creed belong to the truths divinely revealed,[3] what the Church has meant by them requires the "assent of theological

1. Markwart Herzog, "Descensus ad inferos"*: Eine religionsphilosophische Untersuchung der Motive und Interpretationen mit besonderer Berücksichtigung der monographischen Literatur seit dem 16. Jahrhundert,* Frankfurter Theologische Studien 53 (Frankfurt: Josef Knecht, 1997), 243.

2. Alyssa Lyra Pitstick, "Response to Webster and Lauber," *Scottish Journal of Theology*, 62, no. 2 (May 2009): 214-15. This point was elaborated in my presentation to the Karl Barth Society's panel on my book, San Diego, California, Nov. 17, 2007. See also Alyssa Lyra Pitstick, *Light in Darkness: Hans Urs von Balthasar and the Catholic Doctrine of Christ's Descent into Hell* (Grand Rapids: Eerdmans, 2007), 322, 345-46.

3. Congregation for the Doctrine of the Faith, Commentary on the *Professio*, #11.

faith."[4] This is the most fundamental and complete assent of faith possible, what the Profession of Faith calls "firm faith" and Vatican I, "divine and Catholic faith."[5] Such an assent reflects and expresses one's trust in God — and that His revelation is true. Since Christ's descent is part of the creed, the Church's traditional doctrine of it calls for that response of faith.

In contrast, any praise of Balthasar does not. Even less so do his theses on Holy Saturday, which have not been praised by the popes. Indeed, John Paul II has explicitly stated an incompatible position, and Benedict XVI indirectly so.

* * *

In closing, here are the major conclusions of our examination of the evidence provided by the published statements of John Paul II and Ratzinger/Benedict XVI on Christ's descent and on Balthasar, and by thorough study of Balthasar's theology of Holy Saturday (elaborated much more fully in my earlier book, *Light in Darkness*):

1. Balthasar, Ratzinger, and John Paul II have different doctrines of the descent.

According to Balthasar, the Incarnation is suspended with the death of Jesus, and the Son descends as a divine Person denuded of both His natures to a condition far worse than what we call hell. Because all sin comes to exist in His Person there, He suffers its due punishment, the Father's wrath and abandonment. Unbeknownst to Father and Son, the Spirit continues to unite them.

Ratzinger attempted to moderate Balthasar's theology of Holy Saturday, explicitly denying that he could affirm all of it, despite their friendship. Gen-

4. Congregation for the Doctrine of the Faith, Commentary on the *Professio*, #5.

5. For the Profession of Faith, see http://www.vatican.va/roman_curia/congregations/cfaith/documents/rc_con_cfaith_doc_1998_professio-fidei_en.html; for Vatican I, see DS 3011. It would be disingenuous for someone to object that because the Profession uses the Nicene-Constantinopolitan version of the creed (which does not profess Christ's descent explicitly), the Apostles' Creed (which does) is not equally binding. The Apostles' Creed is itself used authoritatively by the Church elsewhere, not least in the CCC. In addition, the Profession also specifies that "everything" the ordinary and universal Magisterium sets forth as divinely revealed is to be held with firm faith, and that certainly includes the Apostles' Creed. In any case, those versions of the creed that, like the Nicene-Constantinopolitan, do not mention the descent explicitly, affirm it implicitly in the articles on the burial and resurrection; see Pitstick, *Light in Darkness*, 9-13.

erally, Ratzinger interpreted the descent as Christ's psychological anguish in the face of death or temptation, with the outcome, however, that Jesus brings His own communion to death's isolation or overcomes temptation with the loving sacrifice of His obedience. Any "abandonment" by God is only apparent.

Ratzinger's themes of Christ's loneliness and apparent abandonment are absent from Benedict XVI, who continues to locate Christ's sufferings before death, though he does not dwell on the nature of those sufferings as much as he did before his election to the papacy. Drawing increasingly upon the psalms and other texts used in the liturgy, Benedict's characterizations of Christ's descent have been more positive, although he has also largely continued to treat them as metaphor. The important exception is his most recent testimony, the television interview in which he indirectly affirmed the realism of the traditional meaning of the Church's profession.

John Paul II consistently affirmed Christ's descent as a real event, in which His sinless soul joined the souls of the just in the limbo of the Fathers and extended His own beatitude to them. The descent thus is the beginning of Christ's manifest glorification.

2. Schönborn does not anticipate the Church's judgment of Balthasar's theology of Holy Saturday, nor does he necessarily reveal his personal opinion.

A negative judgment ultimately seems demanded by the features of the Church's faith which Schönborn acknowledges in his *Introduction to the* Catechism of the Catholic Church (which is a collection of presentations about the CCC and not part of the catechism itself). These points include the affirmation by Sacred Tradition, the likeness of Christ's descent to His resurrection, and the responsibility of the Church to pass on this Tradition. Schönborn's mention of Balthasar by name in his *Introduction* is most likely his response to questions and criticism about particular theologians not appearing in the CCC.

3. A summary standard of the Catholic doctrine of Christ's descent into hell is provided by the *Roman Catechism* and the *Catechism of the Catholic Church,* as articulating God's Revelation transmitted in Scripture and Tradition as interpreted by the Magisterium.

If, as the *Catechism of the Catholic Church* says, with Christ's descent, the gospel message of salvation reaches the dead, to make the saved among them "sharers in the redemption" (#634), then those men and women who died before Christ received the glory of heaven (which is salvation) in His descent. In other words, the *Catechism of the Catholic Church* is consistent (and must be read in that way) with the more explicit *Roman Catechism* in affirming the traditional doctrine.

In its incompatibility with even just these two sources, Balthasar's position is not consistent with Scripture and Tradition as interpreted by the Magisterium.

John Paul II's position possesses just such consistency, however. Indeed, in this very consistency and in his manifest intention to set forth the Church's faith in his catechesis on the creed, John Paul II's exposition of Christ's descent into hell is an exercise of the ordinary *and universal* magisterium. As such, I have argued it is also infallible concerning the realities it affirms. (In short, since the irreformable statements defined by the extraordinary magisterium are not the only exercise of magisterial infallibility, some doctrines — namely, the universal ones — are infallibly taught even if not irreformably expressed as dogma.) At the very least, the doctrines taught in his catechesis are authoritative for Catholics.

Ratzinger's position is somewhere between Balthasar's and John Paul II's. The ambiguity in Ratzinger's expressions can admit compatibility with the Church's doctrine, although the metaphorical "descents" before death he discusses would be more helpfully expressed in other language, especially since the creed itself locates the descent after Christ's death and before His resurrection.

Benedict XVI has indirectly asserted the traditional doctrine. In general, his statements moved in the direction of increasingly explicit affirmations of it.

4. The cardinal's and the popes' praise of Balthasar is not approval of his theology of Holy Saturday.

When examined in the primary sources and not just in secondhand reports, the praise Ratzinger, John Paul II, and Benedict XVI have given Balthasar is neither an exercise of papal infallibility nor even of teaching authority on faith or morals. Neither is it *carte blanche* endorsement nor even approval of any specific idea of his. Indeed, the fact that Ratzinger/Benedict and John Paul II hold positions on Christ's descent incompatible with Balthasar's is implicit criticism on at least that point. The conferral of the Paul VI prize on Balthasar also only acknowledges general features of his theological service, without lauding all his theses or any specific ones.

5. Consequently, arguments that Balthasar has erred do not contradict papal infallibility or authority.

6. On the contrary, to affirm that Christ gloriously shared His own beatitude with the souls of the just who had died before Him when He descended to them in His sinless human soul is to affirm a truth divinely revealed and so one which Christians are called, indeed bound, to believe.

* * *

Critiques of Balthasar's theses will not distress Christians who know their doctrine and their history. Rather, what is scandalous are suggestions to the contrary based either on a careless view of papal authority that exaggerates papal infallibility or on a rejection of the Church's doctrine of the descent.

What happened in Christ's descent? Although all the articles of faith rest on divine revelation, the necessity of such a foundation is particularly evident when an article concerns something beyond the veil of death. Without such revelation, we the living simply have no other way to know what occurs on the other side.

The article on the descent in the creed is not a redundant profession that Christ died. As Christians profess His body was "buried," they profess His soul "descended into hell." This profession does not mean Christ suffered the afterlife's definitive punishment: more recent translations render the article "He descended to the dead" precisely to avoid any such misunderstanding due to the contemporary tendency to use *hell* exclusively in its narrow senses of eternal punishment, suffering, and damnation.

This change in translation reflects the Christian commitment of faith to believe and to preach the truth God has revealed, to confess the meaning of the creed, not just its words. It reflects a desire and a willingness to stand in communion of belief with the cloud of witnesses that goes all the way back to the apostles and back to the beginning. What we believe about Christ's descent consequently is both an act of confidence in God and a bond of union with His Church.

And what has the Church believed? What does Christ's descent in soul to the abode of the dead mean? The *Catechism of the Catholic Church* says that in Christ's descent, salvation reached the ages before the Incarnation. Only realities can bring about realities — and the Catholic faith concerns realities, not mere words. So if real salvation, real perfection of union with God, reached ancient ages, it must have reached real human persons of the past — not humanity in general, but men and women who have names. It reached them through the real presence of Christ among their souls in the afterlife, and it reached them in accord with the real necessity to have died in union with God. For grace in this life is the beginning of glory in the next. The redemption of the world having been completed in the blood of Christ with His death on the cross, the souls of the holy dead received the beatitude of heaven from Christ's own fullness of it during His descent among them, in His human soul united to His divine Person, before His resurrection.

In His descent, Christ faithfully remembers those who were faithful to God during their life. His descent thus also foreshadows the fulfillment of the hope of living believers. Those now united to God by His grace, who believe in Him and keep His commandments, awaiting His return in glory, are in a situation analogous to that of the holy dead at the time of Christ's descent. The living who persevere in His friendship, seeking reconciliation if they fall, will likewise see Him coming one day to bring them into His heavenly glory.

The questions the descent implicitly sets before all the living are questions that were also set before Balthasar, Ratzinger/Benedict XVI, and John Paul II: How does one receive God's revelation? What role does the Church play? Is there a teaching authority in the Church? And finally, how do I choose to relate myself to it?

APPENDIX I

Benedictus Deus' Definition

[Line breaks, emphases, and text in braces have been introduced here to make the distinctions of the definition more manifest.]

2305 (DS 1000) By this Constitution which is to remain in force for ever, we, with apostolic authority, define the following:

According to the general disposition of God,

{1} the souls of all the saints who departed from this world *before the passion* of our Lord Jesus Christ

{2} and also of the holy apostles, martyrs, confessors, virgins and other faithful who died *after receiving* the holy *baptism* of Christ —

provided they were not in need of any purification when they died {applies to 1 and 2},

or will not be in need of any when they die in the future {applies to 2},

or else, if they then needed or will need some purification, after they have been purified after death {applies to 1 and 2} —

{3} and again the souls of children who have been *reborn by the same baptism* of Christ or will be when baptism is conferred on them, if they die before attaining the use of free will:

all these souls {1, 2, and 3},

immediately (*mox*) after death

and, in the case of those in need of purification {applies to 1 and 2}, after the purification mentioned above,

since the ascension of our Lord and Saviour Jesus Christ into heaven,

already before they take up their bodies again and before the general judgment,

have been, are and will be with Christ in heaven, in the heavenly kingdom and paradise, joined to the company of the holy angels.
Since the passion and death of the Lord Jesus Christ,
these souls *have seen and see the divine essence* with an intuitive vision and even face to face, without the mediation of any creature by way of object of vision;
rather the divine essence immediately manifests itself to them, plainly, clearly and openly,
and in this vision they enjoy the divine essence.
Moreover, *by this vision and enjoyment the souls of those who have already died {applies to 1 and to some of 2 and 3} are truly blessed and have eternal life and rest.*
Also the souls of those who will die in the future {applies to some of 2 and 3} will see the same divine essence and will enjoy it before the general judgment.

2306 (DS 1001) Such a vision and enjoyment of the divine essence do away with the acts of faith and hope in these souls,
inasmuch as faith and hope are properly theological virtues.
And after such intuitive and face-to-face vision and enjoyment has or will have begun for these souls,
the same vision and enjoyment has continued and will continue without any interruption and without end until the last Judgment
and from then on forever.

2307 (DS 1002) Moreover we define that according to the general disposition of God,
{4} the souls of those who die in actual mortal sin
go down into hell
immediately (*mox*) after death
and there suffer the pain of hell.
Nevertheless, on the day of judgment
all {1, 2, 3, and 4} will appear with their bodies "before the judgment seat of Christ"
to give an account of their personal deeds,
"so that each one may receive good or evil, according to what one has done in the body" [2 Cor 5:10].

APPENDIX II

Roman Catechism (*Catechism of the Council of Trent*) on Christ's Descent

Article V
"He Descended into Hell, the Third Day He Rose Again from the Dead"

Importance of This Article

To know the glory of the burial of our Lord Jesus Christ, of which we last treated, is highly important; but of still higher importance is it to the faithful to know the splendid triumphs which He obtained by having subdued the devil and despoiled the abodes of hell. Of these triumphs, and also of His Resurrection, we are now about to speak.

Although the latter presents to us a subject which might with propriety be treated under a separate and distinct head, yet following the example of the holy Fathers, we have deemed it fitting to unite it with His descent into hell.

First Part of this Article: "He Descended into Hell"

In the first part of this Article, then, we profess that immediately after the death of Christ His soul descended into hell, and dwelt there as long as His body remained in the tomb; and also that the one Person of Christ was at the same time in hell and in the sepulchre. Nor should this excite surprise; for, as we have already frequently said, although His soul was separated from His body, His Divinity was never parted from either His soul or His body.

"Hell"

As the pastor, by explaining the meaning of the word *hell* in this place may throw considerable light on the exposition of this Article, it is to be observed that by the word *hell* is not here meant the sepulchre, as some have not less impiously than ignorantly imagined; for in the preceding Article we learned that Christ the Lord was buried, and there was no reason why the Apostles, in delivering an Article of faith, should repeat the same thing in other and more obscure terms.

Hell, then, here signifies those secret abodes in which are detained the souls that have not obtained the happiness of heaven. In this sense the word is frequently used in Scripture. Thus the Apostle says: *At the name of Jesus every knee shall bow, of those that are in heaven, on earth, and in hell;*[1] and in the Acts of the Apostles St. Peter says that Christ the Lord is again risen, *having loosed the sorrows of hell.*[2]

Different Abodes Called "Hell"

These abodes are not all of the same nature, for among them is that most loathsome and dark prison in which the souls of the damned are tormented with the unclean spirits in eternal and inextinguishable fire. This place is called *gehenna*, the bottomless pit, and is hell strictly so-called.

Among them is also the fire of purgatory, in which the souls of just men are cleansed by a temporary punishment, in order to be admitted into their eternal country, into which nothing defiled entereth.[3] The truth of this doctrine, founded, as holy Councils declare,[4] on Scripture, and confirmed by Apostolic tradition, demands exposition from the pastor, all the more diligent and frequent, because we live in times when men *endure not sound doctrine*.

Lastly, the third kind of abode is that into which the souls of the just before the coming of Christ the Lord, were received, and where, without experiencing any sort of pain, but supported by the blessed hope of redemption, they enjoyed peaceful repose. To liberate these holy souls, who, in the bosom of Abraham were expecting the Saviour, Christ the Lord descended into hell.

1. Philip. ii. 10.
2. Acts ii. 24.
3. Apoc. xxi. 27.
4. C. of Trent, Sess. xxv.

"He Descended"

We are not to imagine that His power and virtue only, and not also His soul, descended into hell; but we are firmly to believe that His soul itself, really and substantially, descended thither, according to this conclusive testimony of David: *Thou wilt not leave my soul in hell.*[5]

But although Christ descended into hell, His supreme power was in no degree lessened, nor was the splendor of His sanctity obscured by any blemish. His descent served rather to prove that whatever had been foretold of His sanctity was true; and that, as He had previously demonstrated by so many miracles, He was truly the Son of God.

This we shall easily understand by comparing the causes of the descent of Christ with those of other men. They descended as captives; He as free and victorious among the dead, to subdue those demons by whom, in consequence of guilt, they were held in captivity. Furthermore all others descended, either to endure the most acute torments, or, if exempt from other pain, to be deprived of the vision of God, and to be tortured by the delay of the glory and happiness for which they yearned; Christ the Lord descended, on the contrary, not to suffer, but to liberate the holy and the just from their painful captivity, and to impart to them the fruit of His Passion. His supreme dignity and power, therefore, suffered no diminution by His descent into hell.

Why He Descended into Hell

To Liberate the Just

Having explained these things, the pastor should next proceed to teach that Christ the Lord descended into hell, in order that, having despoiled the demons, He might liberate from prison those holy Fathers and the other just souls, and might bring them into heaven with Himself. This He accomplished in an admirable and most glorious manner; for His august presence at once shed a celestial lustre upon the captives and filled them with inconceivable joy and delight. He also imparted to them that supreme happiness which consists in the vision of God, thus verifying His promise to the thief on the cross: *This day thou shalt be with me in paradise.*[6]

This deliverance of the just was long before predicted by Osee in these words:

5. Ps. xv. 10.
6. Luke, xxiii. 43.

O death, I will be thy death; O hell, I will be thy bite;[7] and also by the Prophet Zachary: *Thou also by the blood of thy testament hast sent forth thy prisoners out of the pit, wherein is no water;*[8] and lastly, the same is expressed by the Apostle in these words: *Despoiling the principalities and powers, he hath exposed them confidently in open show, triumphing over them in himself.*[9]

But the better to understand the efficacy of this mystery we should frequently call to mind that not only the just who were born after the coming of our Lord, but also those who preceded Him from the days of Adam, or who shall be born until the end of time, obtain their salvation through the benefit of His Passion. Wherefore before His death and Resurrection heaven was closed against every child of Adam. The souls of the just, on their departure from this life, were either borne to the bosom of Abraham; or, as is still the case with those who have something to be washed away or satisfied for, were purified in the fire of purgatory.

To Proclaim His Power

Another reason why Christ the Lord descended into hell is that there, as well as in heaven and on earth, He might proclaim His power and authority, and that *every knee should bow, of those that are in heaven, on earth, and under the earth.*[10]

And here, who is not filled with admiration and astonishment when he contemplates the infinite love of God for man! Not satisfied with having undergone for our sake a most cruel death, He penetrates the inmost recesses of the earth to transport into bliss the souls whom He so dearly loved and whose liberation from thence He had achieved.[11]

7. Osee xiii. 14.
8. Zach. ix. 11.
9. Col. ii. 15.
10. Phil. ii. 10.
11. On Christ's descent into hell see *Summa Theol.* 3a. lii.

APPENDIX III

Catechism of the Catholic Church on Christ's Descent

ARTICLE 5
"HE DESCENDED INTO HELL. ON THE THIRD DAY HE ROSE AGAIN"

631 Jesus "descended into the lower parts of the earth. He who descended is he who also ascended far above all the heavens."[475] The Apostles' Creed confesses in the same article Christ's descent into hell and his Resurrection from the dead on the third day, because in his Passover it was precisely out of the depths of death that he made life spring forth:

> Christ, that Morning Star, who came back from the dead,
> and shed his peaceful light on all mankind,
> your Son who lives and reigns for ever and ever. Amen.[476]

Paragraph 1. Christ Descended into Hell

632 The frequent New Testament affirmations that Jesus was "raised from the dead" presuppose that the crucified one sojourned in the realm of the dead prior to his resurrection.[477] This was the first meaning given in the apostolic preaching to Christ's descent into hell: that Jesus, like all men, experienced death and in his

475. *Eph* 4:9-10.
476. *Roman Missal,* Easter Vigil 18, *Exsultet.*
477. *Acts* 3:15; *Rom* 8:11; *1 Cor* 15:20; cf. *Heb* 13:20.

soul joined the others in the realm of the dead. But he descended there as Savior, proclaiming the Good News to the spirits imprisoned there.[478]

633 Scripture calls the abode of the dead, to which the dead Christ went down, "hell" – *Sheol* in Hebrew or *Hades* in Greek – because those who are there are deprived of the vision of God.[479] Such is the case for all the dead, whether evil or righteous, while they await the redeemer: which does not mean that their lot is identical, as Jesus shows through the parable of the poor man Lazarus who was received into "Abraham's bosom":[480] "It is precisely these holy souls, who awaited their Savior in Abraham's bosom, whom Christ the Lord delivered when he descended into hell."[481] Jesus did not descend into hell to deliver the damned, nor to destroy the hell of damnation, but to free the just who had gone before him.[482]

634 "The gospel was preached even to the dead."[483] The descent into hell brings the Gospel message of salvation to complete fulfillment. This is the last phase of Jesus's messianic mission, a phase which is condensed in time but vast in its real significance: the spread of Christ's redemptive work to all men of all times and all places, for all who are saved have been made sharers in the redemption.

635 Christ went down into the depths of death so that "the dead will hear the voice of the Son of God, and those who hear will live."[484] Jesus, "the Author of life", by dying destroyed "him who has the power of death, that is, the devil, and [delivered] all those who through fear of death were subject to lifelong bondage."[485] Henceforth the risen Christ holds "the keys of Death and Hades", so that "at the name of Jesus every knee should bow, in heaven and on earth and under the earth."[486]

> Today a great silence reigns on earth, a great silence and a great stillness. A great silence because the King is asleep. The earth trembled and is still

478. Cf. *1 Pet* 3:18-19.
479. Cf. *Phil* 2:10; *Acts* 2:24; *Rev* 1:18; *Eph* 4:9; *Pss* 6:6; 88:11-13.
480. Cf. *Ps* 89:49; *1 Sam* 28:19; *Ezek* 32:17-32; *Lk* 16:22-26.
481. *Roman Catechism* I, 6, 3.
482. Cf. Council of Rome (745): DS 587; Benedict XII, *Cum dudum* (1341): DS 1011; Clement VI, *Super quibusdam* (1351): DS 1077; Council of Toledo IV (625): DS 485; *Mt* 27:52-53.
483. *1 Pet* 4:6.
484. *Jn* 5:25; cf. *Mt* 12:40; *Rom* 10:7; *Eph* 4:9.
485. *Heb* 2:14-15; cf. *Acts* 3:15.
486. *Rev* 1:18; *Phil* 2:10.

because God has fallen asleep in the flesh and he has raised up all who have slept ever since the world began . . . He has gone to search for Adam, our first father, as for a lost sheep. Greatly desiring to visit those who live in darkness and in the shadow of death, he has gone to free from sorrow Adam in his bonds and Eve, captive with him – He who is both their God and the son of Eve . . . "I am your God, who for your sake have become your son . . . I order you, O sleeper, to awake. I did not create you to be a prisoner in hell. Rise from the dead, for I am the life of the dead."[487]

In Brief

636 By the expression "He descended into hell," the Apostles' Creed confesses that Jesus did really die and through his death for us conquered death and the devil "who has the power of death" (*Heb* 2:14).

637 In his human soul united to his divine person, the dead Christ went down to the realm of the dead. He opened heaven's gates for the just who had gone before him.

487. Ancient Homily for Holy Saturday: PG 43, 440A, 452C; *LH*, Holy Saturday, OR.

APPENDIX IV

Pope John Paul II's Catechesis on Christ's Descent

'He Descended into Hell'
General Audience given on January 11, 1989

1. In the most recent reflections we have explained with the help of biblical texts, the article of the Apostles' Creed which says of Jesus "He suffered under Pontius Pilate, was crucified . . . and was buried". It was not merely a case of narrating the history of the Passion, but of penetrating the truth of faith contained in it and which we profess in the Creed: human redemption effected by Christ with his sacrifice. We dwelt particularly on his death and on his words during the agony on the Cross as recorded by the Evangelists. These words help us to discover and understand more profoundly the spirit wherewith Jesus immolated himself for us.

That article of faith ends, as we have just noted, with the words: ". . . and was buried". It might appear a mere factual statement; on the contrary, it is a fact whose significance enters the wider sphere of the whole of Christology. Jesus Christ is the Word made flesh in order to assume the human condition and to be like us in everything except sin (cf. Heb 4:15). He truly became "one of us" (cf. Conc. Vat. II Const. Gaudium et Spes, 22), to be able to redeem us, thanks to the profound solidarity established with every member of the human family. In that condition of true man he experienced completely the lot of man, even to death, which is usually followed by burial, at least in the religious and cultural world in which he lived. Christ's burial is therefore an object of our faith inasmuch as it reproposes for us his mystery of Son of God who became man and ventured to the limit of human experience.

The abode of the dead

2. To these final words of the article on the passion and death of Christ is linked in a certain way the following article which says: "He descended into hell". This article reflects some texts of the New Testament which we shall see shortly. It is well to mention, however, that, although in the time of the Arian controversies the same formula was found in the writings of those heretics, it was nevertheless introduced also into the so-called Creed of Aquileia, one of the professions of the Catholic faith then in use, which was drawn up at the end of the fourth century (cf. DS 16). It entered definitively into the teaching of the Councils with the Fourth Lateran (1215) and the Second Council of Lyons in the profession of faith of Michael Paleologus (1274).

It should also be mentioned straightaway that the word "hell" does not mean the hell of eternal damnation, but the abode of the dead which is "sheol" in Hebrew and "hades" in Greek (cf. Acts 2:31).

3. There are numerous New Testament texts from which the formula is derived. The first is found in the Apostle Peter's discourse of Pentecost. Referring to Psalm 16 to confirm the announcement of Christ's resurrection contained in it, he states that the prophet David "foresaw and spoke of the resurrection of the Christ, that he was not abandoned to Hades, nor did his flesh see corruption" (Acts 2:31). The Apostle Paul's question in the Letter to the Romans has a similar meaning; "'Who will descend into the abyss?' (that is, to bring Christ up from the dead)" (Rom 10:7).

Also in the Letter to the Ephesians there is a text which, in reference to a verse of Psalm 68: "When he ascended on high he led a host of captives, and he gave gifts to men" (Ps 68:18), asks a significant question: "In saying, 'he ascended', what does it mean but that he had also descended into the lower parts of the earth? He who descended is he who also ascended far above all the heavens, so that he might fill all things" (Eph 4:8-10). In this way Paul seems to link Christ's "descent" into the abyss (among the dead), of which he speaks in the Letter to the Romans, with his ascension to the Father, which begins the eschatological "fulfilment" of all things in God.

In line with this are the words placed in Christ's mouth: "I am the First and the Last, and the Living One. I died, and behold I am alive forevermore, and I have the keys of death and Hades" (Rev 1:17-18).

4. As is evident from the texts quoted, the article of the Apostles' Creed, "he descended into hell", is based on the New Testament statements on the descent of

Christ, after his death on the Cross, into the "region of death", into the "abode of the dead", which in Old Testament language was called the "abyss". If the Letter to the Ephesians speaks of "the lower parts of the earth", it is because the earth receives the human body after death, and so it received also the body of Christ who expired on Calvary, as described by the Evangelists (cf. Mt 27:59f and parallel passages; Jn 19:40-42). Christ passed through a real experience of death, including the final moment which is generally a part of the whole process: he was placed in the tomb.

It is a confirmation that this was a real, and not merely an apparent, death. His soul, separated from the body, was glorified in God, but his body lay in the tomb as a corpse.

During the three (incomplete) days between the moment when he "expired" (cf. Mk 15:37) and the resurrection, Jesus experienced the "state of death", that is, the separation of body and soul, as in the case of all people. This is the primary meaning of the words "he descended into hell"; they are linked to what Jesus himself had foretold when, in reference to the story of Jonah, he had said: "For as Jonah was three days and three nights in the belly of the whale, so will the Son of man be three days and three nights in the heart of the earth" (Mt 12:40).

Death and glorification

5. This is precisely what the words about the descent into hell meant: the heart or the womb of the earth. By dying on the cross, Jesus had delivered his spirit into the Father's hands: "Father, into thy hands I commit my spirit!" (Lk 23:46). If death implies the separation of the soul from the body, it follows that in Christ's case also there was, on the one hand, the body in the state of a corpse, and on the other, the heavenly glorification of his soul from the very moment of his death. The First Letter of Peter speaks of this duality when, in reference to Christ's death for sins, he says of him: "Being put to death in the flesh but made alive in the spirit" (1 Pt 3:18). Soul and body are therefore in the final condition corresponding to their nature, although on the ontological plane the soul has a relationship to be reunited with its own body. The Apostle adds however: "In spirit (Christ) went and preached to the spirits in prison" (1 Pt 3:19). This seems to indicate metaphorically the extension of Christ's salvation to the just men and women who had died before him.

6. Obscure as it is, the Petrine text confirms the others concerning the concept of the "descent into hell" as the complete fulfilment of the gospel message of salvation. It is Christ — laid in the tomb as regards the body, but glorified in his soul

admitted to the fullness of the beatific vision of God — who communicates his state of beatitude to all the just whose state of death he shares in regard to the body.

The Letter to the Hebrews describes his freeing of the souls of the just: "Since . . . the children share in flesh and blood, he himself likewise partook of the same nature, that through death he might destroy him who has the power of death, that is, the devil, and deliver all those who through fear of death were subject to lifelong bondage" (Heb 2:14-15). As dead — and at the same time as alive "forevermore"— Christ has "the keys of death and Hades" (cf. Rev 1:17-18). In this is manifested and put into effect the salvific power of Christ's sacrificial death which brought redemption to all, even to those who died before his coming and his "descent into hell", but who were contacted by his justifying grace.

Metaphors of space and time

7. In the First Letter of Peter we read further: ". . . the gospel was preached even to the dead, that though judged in the flesh like men, they might live in the spirit like God" (1 Pt 4:6). This verse also, though not easy to interpret, confirms the concept of the "descent into hell" as the ultimate phase of the Messiah's mission. It is a phase "condensed" into a few days by the texts which try to present in a comprehensible way to those accustomed to reason and to speak in metaphors of space and time, but immensely vast in its real meaning of the extension of redemption to all people of all times and places, even to those who in the days of Christ's death and burial were already in the "realm of the dead". The word of the Gospel and of the Cross reaches all, even those belonging to the most distant generations of the past, because all who have been saved have been made partakers in the Redemption, even before the historical event of Christ's sacrificial death on Calvary took place. The concentration of their evangelization and redemption into the days of the burial emphasizes that in the historical fact of Christ's death there is contained the super-historical mystery of the redemptive causality of Christ's humanity, the "instrument" of the omnipotent divinity. With the entrance of Christ's soul into the beatific vision in the bosom of the Trinity, the "freeing from imprisonment" of the just who had descended to the realm of the dead before Christ, finds its point of reference and explanation. Through Christ and in Christ there opens up before them the definitive freedom of the life of the Spirit, as a participation in the Life of God (cf. St. Thomas, III, q. 52, a. 6). This is the "truth" that can be drawn from the biblical texts quoted and which is expressed in the article of the Creed which speaks of the "descent into hell".

8. We can therefore say that the truth expressed by the Apostles' Creed in the words "he descended into hell", while confirming the reality of Christ's death, at the same time proclaims the beginning of his glorification; and not only of his glorification, but of all those who, by means of his redemptive sacrifice, have been prepared for the sharing in his glory in the happiness of God's Kingdom.

SUPPLEMENT

The Passion and Triumph of Eternal Spring[1]

Spring has sprung! The sky brims with blue. Flower beds ring with blossoms. Rivers leap to kiss and embrace the heights of their earthen banks. The world feels its blood quicken as the crisp air swells our lungs. It practically takes an effort of will to be glum!

Spring's hallmarks of new life are rightly associated with our celebration of the definitive triumph of life over death, the passion and resurrection of Jesus Christ. Yes, the cross is as much a part of his triumph as the empty tomb. By his bodily resurrection, Christ vanquished death, but by his perfect sacrifice of obedient love upon the cross, He conquered sin. By both, He overthrew the reign of the devil, through whose malice sin and death had entered the world. Jesus thus initiated a new Spring for humanity and, indeed, for all creation.

As Christians, we long to enter that definitive Spring. We believe that union with Christ begins that Spring in us and is the way by which we may eventually pass to its full glory. But if Christ's own passover was through the cross and death, then by being united with Him, we must go the same way. Let us look, then, more closely at that way and especially at one overlooked step along it: Christ's descent into hell. For if that descent was part of His passover, then it will also be part of ours.

Motivated by love of the Father and guided by obedience to the divine

1. My thanks and appreciation go to the student editors of *Gonzaga Witness*, whose invitation to write about Christ's descent for their publication led to this piece and whom I saw give such beautiful witness to the joy of a robust Catholic life during my time teaching at Gonzaga University.

will, Jesus's life was one of service to his human brothers and sisters. This service was, first of all, to proclaim the truth about God to all without fear, for it is the response of faith that opens the soul to God's forgiveness and healing: "Your faith has healed you." But since Christ was Himself God's Word, God's truth, His whole life was a proclamation. By His actions, He manifested God's invitation to enter the divine life, together with His desire and work to save man with man's own cooperation. Both were supremely manifested during the Last Supper when Christ gave Himself sacramentally to the Church and, through her, to the world.

Would we follow Jesus into the eternal Spring by way of Holy Thursday, the eve of His passion? Then let us, too, serve all mankind for the love of God and in accord with His will. Let us, too, proclaim without fear the good news of truth and how it sets us free. Let our lives embody Christ and let us remain with Him in the heart of the Church.

One earthly Spring, a fine Friday dawned. That day, the Lamb of God was betrayed, arrested, abandoned, falsely accused, beaten, scourged, mocked, condemned, crucified — all of which would have been absolutely worthless without His love for the Father and for each of us. Perfect love was offered up upon the altar of the cross, and deemed a pleasing sacrifice. It transformed the greatest apparent defeat into the greatest real triumph. If love can thus fill the senseless with significance, the saints were right to say Christ could have redeemed the world with a drop of His blood — and they were right, too, that the abundance He shed manifests the extravagance of His love. "Love covers a multitude of sins," and perfect love washes them clean away from anyone who steps into its flood.

Would we follow Jesus into the eternal Spring by way of Good Friday, the summit of His passion? Then let us, too, prize obedience to God more than the price of our own blood. United to Christ, let us, too, transform all our daily sufferings and the great agonies of life's watershed moments into triumph, even if one recognized only by the eyes of faith. Let our love, as a sharing in Christ's, rise as pleasing incense from the sacrifice of our lives, offered not only for those who love us, but especially for those who harm us. By the miracle of God's grace, may evil works thus not bear evil fruit, but God's own hundredfold fruit of holiness in human hearts.

With the shutting of Christ's eyes in death upon the cross, we come to His descent into hell. Here we must pause a little longer. To modern ears, "hell" denotes the eternal punishment Jesus characterized as a place of flames, wailing, and gnashing of teeth. But it used to be that "hell" could mean any abode of the dead that wasn't heaven. The literal meaning of the word in the creeds is simply "those below." Using physical images to express a spiritual reality, "those below" contrasts the abode of the dead with the heavens "above," which are "the throne of God" (Is 66:1). Before Christ, only God and those God brings to Himself (such as Elijah in the fiery chariot) are "up" in heaven.

Besides the hell of eternal fire, another non-heavenly abode would be purgatory. Some people die in friendship with God, but that friendship still has some rough spots. Purgatory is like a welcome mat: You know you're invited in to the feast, but you have to brush off any remaining dirt first!

Another non-heavenly abode would be for those who didn't die in the state of grace, but also hadn't committed any personal sin. Since punishment after death depends on guilt, these souls wouldn't suffer in what we today call hell. However, because they died without baptism, they also wouldn't have the beatitude to which God invites His adopted children. This abode is called the limbo of the children, or simply limbo. Regardless of debate on the topic, it is a sign of God's mercy: after all, no one *deserves* heaven just because he exists!

The final "hell" was called the limbo of the Fathers. Heaven had been closed after the first sin. Consequently, saintly people who died before Christ had to await the atonement for sin He would accomplish by His death. The Church teaches that this limbo was characterized by peaceful repose.

So what happened in Christ's descent? Being truly human, Jesus died a true human death: His body went to the tomb, while His soul went to an abode of the dead. Both remained united to the Word, however, for Christ's death did not undo His Incarnation. The descent of Christ thus is a descent of the Son of the living God into the realm of death by means of His sinless human soul. Since He was perfectly holy, His soul wouldn't go to the hell of the damned, purgatory, or the limbo of the children. Thus Christ did not suffer in His descent.

Moreover, by His cross, Christ had made perfect union with God possible again. Thus, in His descent, Christ "opened the gates of heaven" to those in the limbo of the Fathers by conferring on them the beatific vision; the noon of eternal Spring filled their souls. Christ descended into hell as a king enters the prison of a conquered castle and sets his faithful servants free. He thus fulfilled His parable about the plundering of the strong man and God's promises that the Christ would enlighten those in darkness and set prisoners free. In the limbo of the Fathers, Christ faithfully remembers those who were faithful to God during their life.

Would we follow Jesus into the eternal Spring by way of Holy Saturday, the firstfruits of His passion? Our union with Christ is imaged in the holy souls in the limbo of the Fathers. We who are *now* united to God by His grace, who *now* believe in Him and keep His commandments, and who *now* await His return in glory are in a position similar to theirs. If we persevere in friendship with God (which includes seeking reconciliation with Him if we fall), then like them, we too shall someday see Him coming to bring us into His heavenly glory!

All this is announced to the world in Christ's resurrection on Easter Sunday. Christ rises from the dead, His wounds made glorious, and ascends bodily to His Father. Sin, death, and the devil hold iron sway no longer; Christ is victor over them all. Jesus's resurrection is His own bodily entrance into the eternal Spring. In Him, the firstborn of many brethren, humanity passes over to eternal life. Thus Easter crowns all earthly Springs regardless of the date it falls upon. United to Christ, we look forward in hope to our own resurrection into heaven after death and our resurrection in the body on the Last Day. Then shall our lungs swell with the pure breath of the Spirit, our eyes delight in the light of perfect truth, and our hearts and blood run warm with the sunfire of God's love.

> My beloved speaks and says to me: "Arise, my love, my fair one, and come away; for lo, the winter is past, the rain is over and gone. The flowers appear on the earth, the time of singing has come . . ." (Song of Songs 2:10-12).

BIBLIOGRAPHY

Abbott, S.J., Walter M., ed. *The Documents of Vatican II.* New York: America, 1966.

Aquinas, St. Thomas. *Summa Theologiae.*

Balthasar, Hans Urs von. "Abstieg zur Hölle." In *Pneuma und Institution.*

———. *The Action.* Vol. 4 of *Theo-Drama.* Translated by Graham Harrison. San Francisco: Ignatius, 1994.

———. *Church and World.* Translated by A. V. Littledale with Alexander Dru. New York: Herder & Herder, 1967.

———. "Death Is Swallowed up by Life." *Communio ICR* 14, no. 2 (1987): 49-54.

———. "The Descent into Hell." In *Spirit and Institution.*

———. *The Dramatis Personae: The Person in Christ.* Vol. 3 of *Theo-Drama.* Translated by Graham Harrison. San Francisco: Ignatius, 1992.

———. *Elucidations.* Translated by John Riches. San Francisco: Ignatius, 1975.

———. *The God Question and Modern Man.* Translated by Hilda Graef. New York: Seabury, 1967.

———. "Kenosis of the Church?" In *Spirit and Institution.*

———. *The Last Act.* Vol. 5 of *Theo-Drama.* Translated by Graham Harrison. San Francisco: Ignatius, 1998.

———. *Leben aus dem Tod: Betrachtungen zum Ostermysterium.* Einsiedeln: Johannes, 1997.

———. "Loneliness in the Church." In *Spirit and Institution.*

———. *Mysterium Paschale: The Mystery of Easter.* Translated by Aidan Nichols. Edinburgh: T. & T. Clark, 1990.

———. "On Vicarious Representation." In *Spirit and Institution.*

———. *Pneuma und Institution.* Bd. IV, *Skizzen zur Theologie.* Einsiedeln: Johannes, 1974.

———. "Scapegoat and the Trinity." In *You Crown the Year with Your Goodness.*

———. "Some Points of Eschatology." In *The Word Made Flesh.*

———. *Spirit and Institution.* Explorations in Theology 4. Translated by Edward T. Oakes. San Francisco: Ignatius, 1995.

———. *Theology: The New Covenant.* Vol. 7 of *The Glory of the Lord: A Theological Aesthetics.* Translated by Brian McNeil. Edited by John Riches. San Francisco: Ignatius, 1984.

———. "Trinity and Future." In *Elucidations.*

———. *The Word Made Flesh.* Explorations in Theology 1. Translated by A. V. Littledale and Alexander Dru. San Francisco: Ignatius, 1989.

———. *You Crown the Year with Your Goodness.* Translated by Graham Harrison. San Francisco: Ignatius, 1989.

———. "Zur Frage: 'Hoffnung für alle': Eine Antwort auf den Artikel von Pfr. Karl Besler." *Theologisches* 199 (1986): 7363-66.

Benedict XVI. Address on the Occasion of His Visit to the Auschwitz Camp. May 28, 2006.

———. Easter Vigil Homily. April 7, 2007.

———. General Audience. September 14, 2011.

———. General Audience. February 8, 2012.

———. General Audience. February 15, 2012.

———. "Intervista a Benedetto XVI." Programma "A Sua Immagine. Domande su Gesù." Rai Uno. April 22, 2011. Transcript at http://www.vatican.va/holy_father/benedict_xvi/speeches/2011/april/documents/hf_ben-xvi_spe_20110422_intervista_it.html, accessed most recently April 9, 2013.

———. "Message to the Participants in the International Convention on the Occasion of the Centenary of the Birth of the Swiss Theologian Hans Urs von Balthasar." October 6, 2005. Translated at http://www.communio-icr.com/articles/BenedictBalthasarCentenary.html, accessed April 9, 2011.

———. Messagio. October 6, 2005.

———. "Seven Questions for the Pope." Catholic News Service. April 22, 2011. Transcript at http://cnsblog.wordpress.com/2011/04/22/seven-questions-for-the-pope/, accessed April 26, 2011.

———. *Spe salvi (Saved by Hope).* November 30, 2007.

———. "Veneration of the Holy Shroud Meditation." May 2, 2010.

Catechism of the Catholic Church. New Hope, KY: Urbi et Orbi Communications, 1994.

Catechism of the Council of Trent. Translated by John A. McHugh, O.P., and Charles J. Callan, O.P. Rockford, IL: Tan, 1982.

Clement XIII. *In Dominico Agro (On Instruction in the Faith).* June 14, 1761. Reproduced at http://www.papalencyclicals.net/Clem13/c13indom.htm, accessed August 20, 2012.

Congregation for the Doctrine of the Faith. Commentary on the Concluding Formula of the *Professio Fidei.* June 29, 1998. http://www.vatican.va/

roman_curia/congregations/cfaith/documents/rc_con_cfaith_doc_1998_professio-fidei_en.html.

———. "The Primacy of the Successor of Peter in the Mystery of the Church." October 31, 1998.

Cooper, Alan. "Ps 24:7-10: Mythology and Exegesis." *Journal of Biblical Literature* 102, no. 1 (1983): 37-60.

Dulles, S.J., Avery. *Magisterium: Teacher and Guardian of the Faith.* Naples, FL: Sapientia, 2007.

Dupuis, Jacques, ed. *The Christian Faith in the Doctrinal Documents of the Catholic Church.* 6th ed. Staten Island, NY: Alba House, 1996.

Grillmeier, Alois. "Der Gottessohn im Totenreich: Soteriologische und christologische Motivierung der Descensuslehre in der älteren christlichen Überlieferung." In *Mit ihm und in ihm: Christologische Forschungen und Perspektiven.* 2. Auflage, 76-174. Freiburg: Herder, 1975.

Herzog, Markwart. "Descensus ad inferos": *Eine religionsphilosophische Untersuchung der Motive und Interpretationen mit besonderer Berücksichtigung der monographischen Literatur seit dem 16. Jahrhundert.* Frankfurter Theologische Studien 53. Frankfurt: Josef Knecht, 1997.

Istituto Paolo VI. *Hans Urs von Balthasar: Premio Internazionale Paolo VI, 1984.* Brescia: Istituto Paolo VI, 1984.

John XXII. *Ne super his.* Dec. 3, 1334.

John Paul II. *Ad tuendam fidem.* May 18, 1998.

———. *Catechesi Tradendae.* October 16, 1979.

———. "Il Discorso del Santo Padre Giovanni Paolo II." In Istituto Paolo VI, *Hans Urs von Balthasar: Premio Internazionale Paolo VI, 1984*, 9-13.

———. *Fidei depositum.* October 11, 1992.

———. General Audience. June 20, 2001.

———. General Audience. April 3, 1996.

———. General Audience. January 11, 1989. Translated by *L'Osservatore Romano Weekly Edition in English.* January 16, 1989.

———. General Audience. December 7, 1988.

———. General Audience. November 30, 1988.

———. General Audience. October 26, 1988.

———. General Audience. October 19, 1988.

———. Omelia. March 29, 1986.

———. "Telegram." *Communio* 15, no. 4 (1988): 511.

Jordan, Mark, ed. *The Church's Confession of Faith: A Catholic Catechism for Adults.* Translated by Stephen Wentworth Arndt. San Francisco: Ignatius, 1987.

Keating, Karl. *Catholicism and Fundamentalism: The Attack on "Romanism" by "Bible Christians."* San Francisco: Ignatius Press, 1998.

Leo XIII. *Dépuis le jour.* September 8, 1899.

Lubac, Henri de. "A Witness to Christ in the Church: Hans Urs von Balthasar." *Communio* 2, no. 3 (Fall, 1975).

"La Motivazione del Premio." In Istituto Paolo VI, *Hans Urs von Balthasar: Premio Internazionale Paolo VI, 1984*.

Oakes, S.J., Edward T. "*Descensus* and Development: A Response to Recent Rejoinders." *International Journal of Systematic Theology* 13, no. 1 (January, 2011): 3-24.

Ott, Ludwig. *Fundamentals of Catholic Dogma*. Translated by Patrick Lynch. Rockford, IL: Tan, 1974.

Pitstick, Alyssa Lyra. "Development of Doctrine, or Denial? Balthasar's Holy Saturday and Newman's *Essay*." *International Journal of Systematic Theology* 11, no. 2 (April, 2009): 129-45.

———. *Light in Darkness: Hans Urs von Balthasar and the Catholic Doctrine of Christ's Descent into Hell*. Grand Rapids: Eerdmans, 2007.

———. "Response to Webster and Lauber." *Scottish Journal of Theology* 62, no. 2 (May, 2009): 211-16.

Pitstick, Alyssa Lyra, and Edward T. Oakes, S.J. "Balthasar, Hell, and Heresy: An Exchange." *First Things* (December, 2006): 25-32.

———. "More on Balthasar, Hell, and Heresy." *First Things* (January, 2007): 16-19.

———. "Responses to 'Balthasar, Hell, and Heresy.'" *First Things* (March, 2007): 5-14.

Pius XII. *Munificentissimus Deus*. November 1, 1950.

Ratzinger, Joseph. *Behold the Pierced One*. Translated by Graham Harrison. San Francisco: Ignatius, 1986.

———. *Dogma and Preaching: Applying Christian Doctrine to Daily Life*. Translated by Matthew J. O'Connell. Chicago: Franciscan Herald, 1985.

———. *Einführung in das Christentum: Vorlesungen über das Apostolische Glaubensbekenntnis*. Munich: Kösel, 2000.

———. *Eschatologie: Tod und ewiges Leben*. Vol. 9 of Johann Auer and Joseph Ratzinger, *Kleine Katholische Dogmatik*. Regensburg: Pustet, 1977.

———. "Five Meditations." In *The Sabbath of History*.

———. *From the Baptism in the Jordan to the Transfiguration*. Vol. 1 of *Jesus of Nazareth*. Translated by Adrian J. Walker. New York: Doubleday, 2007.

———. *God Is Near Us: The Eucharist, the Heart of Life*. San Francisco: Ignatius, 2003.

———. *Holy Week: From the Entrance into Jerusalem to the Resurrection*. Vol. 2 of *Jesus of Nazareth*. Translated by Philip J. Whitmore. San Francisco: Ignatius, 2011.

———. "Homily at the Funeral Liturgy for Hans Urs von Balthasar." *Communio ICR* 15 (Winter, 1988): 512-16.

———. "Homilie beim Gedenkgottesdienst für Hans Urs von Balthasar." *Internationale katholische Zeitschrift Communio* 17, no. 1 (January, 1988): 473-76.

———. *The Sabbath of History*. Washington, DC: William G. Congdon Foundation, 2000.

———. *The Spirit of the Liturgy*. San Francisco: Ignatius, 2000.

Ratzinger, Joseph, and Christoph Schönborn. *Introduction to the* Catechism of the Catholic Church. Translated by Adrian Walker. San Francisco: Ignatius, 1994.

Roman Catechism. See *Catechism of the Council of Trent.*

Rufinus. *A Commentary on the Apostles' Creed.* Translated by W. H. Fremantle. Nicene and Post-Nicene Fathers 2nd ser. 3. Grand Rapids: Eerdmans, 1979.

Schönborn, Christoph. "A Short Introduction to the Four Parts of the Catechism." In Ratzinger and Schönborn, *Introduction to the* Catechism of the Catholic Church.

———. "Major Themes and Underlying Principles of the Catechism of the Catholic Church." In Ratzinger and Schönborn, *Introduction to the* Catechism of the Catholic Church.

Sheed, Frank. *Theology and Sanity.* San Francisco: Ignatius, 1993.

Spicq, C. "La Révélation de l'Enfer dans la Sainte Écriture." In *L'Enfer*, 89-143. Foi Vivante 52. Paris: Les Éditions de la Revue des Jeunes, 1950.

Vatican II. *Dei Verbum.* Dogmatic Constitution on Divine Revelation. Nov. 18, 1965.

———. *Gaudium et spes.* Pastoral Constitution on the Church in the Modern World. In Abbott, ed., *The Documents of Vatican II.*

Vogels, Heinz-Jürgen. *Christi Abstieg ins Totenreich und das Läuterungsgericht an den Toten.* Freiburger Theologische Studien 120. Freiburg: Herder, 1976.

Wicks, S.J., Jared. "Christ's Saving Descent to the Dead: Early Witnesses from Ignatius of Antioch to Origen." *Pro Ecclesia* 17, no. 3 (Summer, 2008): 281-310.

Wuerl, Donald W. *The Catholic Way: Faith for Living Today*. New York: Doubleday, 2011.